D0460129

REVOLUTION

WITHIN

DWIGHT EDWARDS

WATERBROOK
PRESS

REVOLUTION WITHIN

PUBLISHED BY WATERBROOK PRESS

2375 Telstar Drive, Suite 160

Colorado Springs, Colorado 80920

A division of Random House, Inc.

ISBN 1-57856-459-X

Published in association with Yates & Yates, LLP, Literary Agent, Orange, California

Library of Congress Cataloging-in-Publication Data

Edwards, Dwight, 1954–
    Revolution within : a fresh look at supernatural living / by Dwight Edwards.—1st ed.
    p. cm.
    Includes bibliographical references.
    ISBN 1-57856-459-X
    I. Christian life.   I. Title.

BV4501.3 .E39 2001
248.4—dc21   2001017536

Printed in the United States of America

2003

10   9   8   7

To my beloved wife, Sandy,
whose vibrant, grace-soaked life
has taught me so much about the New Covenant

Contents

Let Your Heart Dream

Is it really possible that before Christ returns His Spirit may once again move in revival power? Might there be another Great Awakening that stirs the church to first tremble before God and then pant after Him?

It would take deep brokenness, something we've trivialized into merely facing the wounds from our past. And it would require repentance, which to many moderns means little more than admitting we need help and going for counseling.

If we faced how shallow and powerless our lives have become, how self-absorbed and ruled by a spirit of entitlement we actually are, perhaps we would be transformed from a community of the comfortable (or at least trying to be) into the community of the broken. And if that happened, maybe the Spirit would continue His work by turning us into a community of hope, men and women praying fervently for another "time of refreshing" from the Lord.

Our weighty God is right now sitting lightly on His church. To the watching world, He must seem more a shiny veneer decorating our lives than our sure foundation. Good things, of course, are happening—the Spirit is faithfully building Christ's church—but as one pastor recently put it to me: "Something's missing. I see obvious blessing and I know it's God's hand. But sometimes I envision what the Spirit must long to do in God's people and I wonder if anything real is happening at all. I know it is, but there could be so much more."

I wonder if any of us look at Christ and, in the middle of terrible trial, say He is enough, and mean it? Or watch cherished dreams shatter and with renewed vigor pursue the greater dream of knowing Him better, and do so with gratitude for the privilege? Do any of us know what it is to suffer betrayal and rejection and count it all joy, not only that we're deemed worthy to suffer for the name but also that now we have unique opportunity to reveal what Christ is like to our abusers? Do we value knowing God and glorifying Him—no matter what's happening in our lives—more than depending on God and using Him to make our lives more fulfilling?

I worry that we've twisted the message of the Cross into a promise that God will provide us enough creature comforts on earth, whether material or spiritual, to keep the journey to heaven reasonably pleasant till we get there. We think it's His job to see to it that we feel pretty good here till we feel forever good there. Modern Christianity, in dramatic reversal of its biblical form, is now all about us.

God hasn't checked with me on this (nor on anything else), but I sense that He may be setting the stage for another *reformation* that, coupled with true *revival*, could spark a *revolution* in the church.

The first reformation recovered with liberating clarity the truth of *how* we're made right with God, how we receive God's life and the guarantee of enjoying it forever. I suggest that the reformation needed in the church today would focus on *why* God gives us life, on the real reason that Jesus died. "It is not for your sake…that I am going to do these things," God said, "but for the sake of my holy name."

The Spirit would cut through our narcissistic nuttiness to make clear that God saved us in order for Him to receive glory, not to help us feel good about ourselves and lead exciting lives. We would see that Christ's blood was shed so that, as forgiven disciples, we might trust God when life falls apart rather than expecting Him to keep it together. Light would dispel the fog that prevents us from seeing anything beyond our own longings, and we would realize that life—our relationships, our health, our bank accounts, our time—is not all about us. *It's all about God.* He's the star of the show. We would see that we're bit players, and we'd be thrilled that we're part of the drama. No suffering would be viewed as unfair for us to endure if it helped keep the spotlight on Christ. That would be a turnabout, a reformation in our understanding of what God is up to in the gospel.

Revival would follow. The Spirit would convince us that under the terms of God's new arrangement with people—the New Covenant brought in at Pentecost that replaced the old one begun at Sinai—God has done more than we think. We've not only been forgiven so completely that the Father now sings over us with delight at every moment from conversion on, but He has also changed us, deeply, profoundly, permanently. Under the new arrangement we're not merely ordered to glorify God, we now *want* to. And we're equipped to do it. It becomes actually possible, we see it as our highest privilege and joy, to revolve our lives around God.

We discover an appetite within us that prefers the pleasures of holiness to the pleasures of sin. With Augustine, we actually experience the joy of knowing God's love as greater than the very real fun of sexual release—and so we overcome our addictions and express our sexuality within moral boundaries. We experience the pleasure of His company and the privilege of being in His service as far surpassing all lesser pleasures and privileges. And so we mature; we become more like Christ. We lead changed (though still imperfect) lives that reveal a new power in our makeup that puzzles people who watch.

We were saved to glorify God. Realizing that one truth is the heart of the reformation that the modern church must experience. And our salvation provides us with all the resources we need to pull it off. That realization and learning how to draw on those resources will begin the revival. Our lives can actually be all about God and not about us. That's the coming revolution.

Think about it. Let your heart dream. From narcissists to worshipers. From people trying hard to make our lives more pleasing to us, to people who make it our priority to please God. Men would turn off their cable pornography. Lonely women would no longer date still-married men. People with limited means would be glad when their friends become rich. Children would spend time with their aging parents and count it a privilege to do so. We'd stop being so damnably selfish and actually be more concerned for others than for ourselves, even when the price is high. The church would shift from a fractious society of ego-driven competitors whose souls never meet to a gathering of broken, grateful saints ruled by the passion of grace. We'd become a *community.*

If the Spirit reforms our understanding of why God bothered to save us in the first place, if He revives our passion to live sacrificially for Him without focusing on our own immediate sense of well-being, a revolution will be set in motion. The church will be on its way to again being the church, never perfectly of course, but perhaps as substantially as in the days of Acts.

The book you're about to read could trigger that revolution. *Revolution Within,* written by my close friend and colleague Dwight Edwards, is well titled. With the passion of a man on a mission from God and with the power of a writer who listens to the Spirit as his fingers move across the keyboard, Dwight in this book lays the foundation for both reformation and revival, the reformation and revival the modern church desperately needs.

I remember when he called me from his home in Texas to say, "Larry, something just hit me. God introduced the New Covenant to pull His name out of the mud. I've read it before in Ezekiel—it's plain as day—but now I see it. The gospel is all about God's glory; it's not about my fulfillment. But living for His glory guarantees my fulfillment!" He was nearly shouting.

Another call, a few months later: "I'm realizing that the gospel actually changes who we are, not just our legal position before God. The pressure's off! Now I can glorify God by releasing who I really am. Larry, we've missed the thrill of New Covenant living. It's far better than most of us have ever imagined. I thought my job as a pastor was to persuade people to do what they really didn't want to do and to act like people they really weren't. But my calling is to tell them what God has done, stir up their holy appetites, provide some basic direction, and turn 'em loose."

Read this book. Give a copy to your friends. It's all about theology. But you'll think it's an exciting story. Of course that's what theology is. It's the exciting story of God—who He is and what He's doing, especially with us.

Don't just read it, though. Open your heart to the Spirit as you slowly turn its pages. This book may jump-start the revolution you've longed for in yourself, in your small group, and in your church. As never before, you may experience supernatural living, a life that's all about God and a freedom to live out who you really are, a lover of God. The revolution within has already happened. This book will make that clear. After digesting its message, you'll want to make the revolution visible.

—DR. LARRY CRABB

Falling in Line with Your True Design

There's a Native American fable about a young brave who happened upon a nest of golden eagle eggs. Deciding to have some fun, he took one of the eggs and placed it in the nest of some prairie chickens.

The egg hatched, and the changeling eagle grew up with the brood of prairie chickens. Believing himself to be like everyone else around him, he behaved accordingly. He clucked and cackled and scratched in the dirt for seeds and insects to live on. He never flew more than a few feet off the ground, since prairie chickens are incapable of rising any higher.

Years passed. One day the young eagle was scratching along with one of his older prairie chicken brothers when a fleeting shadow passed over them. They looked up and saw, high in the sky, the soaring form of something gliding on the currents of the wind.

"What a beautiful bird!" the young eagle exclaimed.

"That's an eagle," the older brother informed him, staring upward. "A golden eagle. He's the king of the air. No bird can compare with him." Then he lowered his gaze and added, "But don't give it a second thought; you could never be like him."

And back to scratching they went. Indeed, the changeling eagle never gave another thought to that soaring sight. According to the fable, he died as he had lived, never rising any higher than a prairie chicken's existence.

Tragically, this same story is repeated in the lives of far too many believers. Like eagles, we were created and redeemed to mount up on God-given wings. Our privileged calling is to breathe deeply the crisp and rarified air of knowing our God more and more intimately…to know the keen thrill of unrestrained, exuberant worship…and to abandon ourselves to the high adventure of warring on behalf of God's kingdom in this dark world.

This is our God-given design—and that's why we cannot truly be satisfied with anything less. We can never find the intense fulfillment our souls yearn for while scratching around in carnal living or mediocre spirituality. We were made—*and fully equipped at the time of our conversion*—to soar.

What we'll explore in this book is simply the abiding joy of falling in line with our true design. We'll discover many surprising and life-changing realities, to the glory of God, whose lavish grace makes this kind of soaring truly attainable.

We'll see more clearly how amazing God's grace really is—not just in how He redeemed us, but even more in the quality of day-to-day living that He both invites us to and fully outfits us for.

GOD'S SAFETY NET

During the initial stages of constructing the famous Golden Gate Bridge, twenty-three workers fell to their deaths in the cold waters connecting the North Pacific with San Francisco Bay. Finally, halfway through the project, a large net was put in place beneath the bridge. Surprisingly, from then on only ten men actually fell—all safely caught by the net. Beyond this, there was a full 25 percent increase in the workers' productivity rate. Assured that their safety was no longer in question, they pursued their work with far greater freedom and effectiveness than before.

This is exactly what God has done for us. Stretched wide beneath us, extending from eternity past to eternity future, is God's perfect grace, assuring every believer that we can never fall from His favor. No matter how badly we falter or fail, we can never plunge past the grace of God. In this book we'll seek to bring into sharper awareness the undiluted, unrestricted flow of His grace into our daily lives. As we do so, we'll discover the delightfully unexpected result in what it does for our purity and godly living.

We'll also explore one of the most powerful yet overlooked *motivations* for such godly living, and one of the most liberating truths I've ever learned. It's the great reality that the desire to do the will of God is the gift of God. I spent so many years trying to muster up desire for what I knew God was requiring of me, or praying that God would change my heart. The good news, as we'll thoroughly investigate in these pages, is that *God has already changed* my heart, and yours as well.

HERE'S YOUR STEAK

For many years, as a pastor and teacher, I taught with the basic assumption that most of the people in front of me didn't really want to obey God's will. It was my job to try to coerce them into doing what they fundamentally didn't want to do. I call it now the "eat your vegetables" approach to ministry: You may not like what

God commands, but go ahead and do it anyway because it's good for you.

Now I work from the basic assumption that, deep down, every true believer *does* want to do the will of God—though so many are unaware of this or are blocked in that realization. Now I try to minister from a "here's your steak" approach, helping others see all that they were created for and enticing the new appetite for righteousness that God placed in their souls at conversion.

We'll also behold the liberating truth that God gives us not only a new set of "want tos" for doing His will, but also a new "can do" through His Spirit to actually carry out our new inclinations.

As we more fully recognize our new purity, our new identity, our new disposition, and our new power, we'll explore their divinely intended results: new intimacy with God, new liberty in daily living, a new community with other believers, and a new ministry through the Spirit.

So come, my friend, let's learn more about this new reality that God has called us to…that He's deeply inclined our hearts toward…and that He's also fully empowered us to carry out.

CHAPTER 1

Ready for Release

Discipleship is built entirely on the supernatural grace of God.

OSWALD CHAMBERS

Many Christians view their conversion as something like a car wash: You go in a filthy clunker; you come out with your sins washed away—a cleansed clunker.

Such cleansing indeed happened when we became Christians, but *so much more* transpired as well! It's as if, right there between the power wash and power rinse cycles, a brand new engine was dropped into the car, plus entirely new wiring. Of course the old engine is temporarily left in, and we can choose (foolishly) to operate by it and to live like the clunker we were. But *we don't have to*— because of a revolution that's happened within us.

It's a revolution we learn more about in what I believe are some of the most powerful yet badly neglected realities in all the Word of God.

THE GUN AT MY HEAD

One day about fifteen years ago I was chatting with a friend and gifted counselor, and he made this observation: "Dwight, you live with the word *should* pointed to your head like a gun." I honestly didn't know at the time if this was a compliment or a rebuke. After all, the key to the Christian life, as best I understood it, was commitment and obedience—carrying out all the "shoulds" that Scripture is filled with.

Another word that described my spiritual life in those days was *pressured.* I was seeking to live up to the vast array of God's standards that seemed to press down on me relentlessly. Most of the standards I held for myself were totally legitimate and based on the Word of God. But what I'd never heard before in any substantive fashion was the staggering news that *God* has provided us with the "wants" for His "shoulds."

God used that conversation with my friend, plus a tape series on "Freedom" by Larry Crabb, to launch me on my own pilgrimage into what the Bible calls the New Covenant. Along the way I've continued to discover a hope for present Christian living that I never knew existed. Perplexing verses such as "His commandments are not burdensome"* have begun to make sense. I discovered that through the New Covenant the burden is lifted because of the new disposition and new power God has given for carrying out His standards.

I have far, far to go in fully appropriating this reality; on this earth I always will. But the little ground God has allowed me to cover has deeply convinced me that there is a genuine rest of soul, a joyfulness of spirit, and an unpressured spirituality that come only through the wondrous provisions of the New Covenant.

So What's New?

If you're thinking, *So what's the big deal about the New Covenant?* I can identify. I spent many years as a believer and even as a pastor

---

* References for all quoted Scripture passages are listed in the back of this book.

thinking I knew pretty well what the New Covenant was all about: Jesus shedding His blood for our sins and justifying us by His righteousness. What I hadn't realized was how much *more* the New Covenant provided.

I've now seen time and again how much difference this "more" really does make in everyday life. New Covenant truths—which deal more with how we *live* than how we're saved—are not just theological jargon but life-changing, eagle-soaring realities.

Late one night I received a visit from Greg, a twenty-five-year-old single who had been growing in his faith for several years. That day, however, he'd given in to homosexual urges that seemed to overwhelm him.

I'll never forget the look of anguish and desperation etched upon his face that night as he described the intensity of the battle raging within. There was no question in his mind that what he'd done was wrong, that he hated that part of himself, that he would dearly love to be free from these wayward longings. But they were so unbearably strong that he honestly wondered if he had any hope of substantial change.

I was deeply perplexed over what to tell Greg. He was a committed believer sincerely pursuing Christ. He was already doing most of the prescribed disciplines for godliness—quiet time, Scripture memory, prayer, Bible study, fellowship, sharing his faith, involvement in ministry. Yet, in his greatest hour of need, they all seemed impotent to restrain his sin. Why didn't the gospel have more power in the life of one who truly wanted to change? What would it take to fix Greg in this area?

This same scenario is repeated daily in thousands of forms— the mother whose quick temper erupts all too frequently toward her children, the husband who can't shake free from the chains of pornography, the pastor who cannot overcome his bitterness toward a board member, the teenager who violates his conscience for the approval of his peers. All of us have areas in our lives where we recognize an undeniable chasm between knowing what we should do and actually doing it. The answer to fixing these faults continues to elude us.

Not Fixing, but Releasing

True breakthroughs will never come, however, if we keep working to get ourselves "fixed." They will come only as we embark on a completely new journey.

That journey is what this book is all about. It's an expedition focused not on fixing, but releasing.

Let me tell you more about Greg, who came to me in such desperation. Today he's happily married, a wonderful father, walking closely with God, and having significant ministry in his job and church. Does he ever face temptation toward homosexuality? Yes, but not nearly as much. Greg is a wonderful example of what Francis Schaeffer called "substantial healing." His transformation isn't total (no one's is, this side of eternity), but it is very, very substantial. There were a number of things God used in his life to help bring about this healing, including good counseling, loving friends, and a helpful church. But Greg would tell you that far and away the most important was this: *the discovery, appropriation, and release of the divine resources provided through the New Covenant.*

Knowing and releasing these resources has strengthened and sustained me in my own spiritual pilgrimage time and again. Certainly I continue to battle daily with my flesh. There are times when I feel so overwhelmed by guilt, lust, fear, or anger that I wonder if I'll ever get past my perverse sin nature. But through the New Covenant I've discovered the good news of *another reality*—that beneath all my sin, all the dysfunction of my past, all my insecurities, all my rebellion, there resides a radical new nature, implanted and sustained by God alone. Sometimes that new nature seems elusive, especially when it's covered over by other competing passions. But just because it doesn't seem real doesn't mean it isn't real. Because of the New Covenant, I know God has infused me with a new nature of His own making that can never be diminished or removed.

That's why the great issue in Christian living is not how to get ourselves fixed but *how to get our new nature released.*

So Hard to Let Go

With that in mind, let's try to understand more practically what the Bible means by the term *New Covenant.*

The word *covenant* is used often in Scripture for God's dealings or arrangements with man, such as certain agreements He made with Noah, Abraham, and David. One especially significant covenant he made was with Moses and the nation of Israel after they came out of Egypt. This so-called Old Covenant is also known throughout Scripture as "the law."

But later we encounter what God calls "a new covenant," promised through the Old Testament prophets and taught more fully in our New Testament. From the first mention of it, God states that it will be wholly unlike the law. This new arrangement, He emphasizes, is "not according to" the old one. In fact its two sharpest distinctives are its *radical difference* from the law, and its *radical superiority* to it.

And why should that concern us?

Because it's harder than most of us think to fully let go of a law-based approach to spirituality. Our flesh naturally gravitates toward legalistic approaches to holiness that encourage at least some reliance on self. A blend of God's helping us and our helping God is both reasonable and enticing to our fallen nature. It enables us to partially share credit with God for any spiritual success. Most of all, it keeps our pride at least somewhat intact.

MAKE A CLEAN BREAK

But what's really so wrong about mixing a little Old Covenant into our lives? Won't it cause people to live more fully for God?

The New Testament warns us, however, to give up law-based spirituality or suffer significant spiritual consequences. True spirituality requires an absolutely clean break from the old way of doing things, replacing it with a radically new approach to God-honoring living.

Jesus had this in mind when He said,

No one sews a piece of unshrunk cloth on an old garment;
or else the new piece pulls away from the old, and the tear is
made worse. And no one puts new wine into old wineskins;
or else the new wine bursts the wineskins, the wine is spilled,
and the wineskins are ruined. But new wine must be put
into new wineskins.

Here He makes two highly significant points concerning His relationship with the old system, the law.

First, *Jesus did not come to patch up the Old Covenant.* He brought in a brand new garment, not a stitch job on an old one.

Second, *Jesus did not come to fit into the old system, but to cleanly replace it.* Like new wine, He is too powerful and vibrant to be confined by the old.

In both cases the message is this: If you mingle these two realities—Old and New Covenants—you end up ruining the whole lot. It's like mixing diesel with regular gas in your car; at best, it will only sputter. The New Covenant doesn't try to salvage what it can from the old, but cleanly replaces it with the new.

Is there some sputtering because of a wrong mix in your spiritual engine? Or does your life impart the supernatural outflow of the indwelling life of Christ, which is the essence of the New Covenant? Let me say it again: *The normal Christian life is nothing more or less than the outflowing of the indwelling Christ.*

"NO THROWING ROCKS"

This is why the key to the Christian life is *not* obedience to God's standards.

That statement may sound like out-and-out heresy to you, so let me hasten to say that obedience to God's standards is a hugely important part of Christian living. One cannot honestly read the Scriptures without coming to this conclusion. But in true spirituality, obedience to God's standards is the by-product and inevitable result of something that's centrally more important.

One of the main reasons the obedience demanded by the law could not produce spirituality in God's people is the effect law has on our flesh. Years ago I was camping beside a river. I'd been there only a few minutes when I saw a sign: "No Throwing Rocks into the River." Guess what? Suddenly I was overcome with a tremendous urge to throw at least one rock into the river. It never even occurred to me to throw a rock until I read that sign, but the law of the campsite aroused the rebellion in my flesh. (I'll leave you guessing as to whether I actually threw it.)

When God's standards press down upon us, our flesh naturally rises up in rebellion. Paul notes that our "sinful passions...were aroused by the law." Ever since the Fall, our flesh has been hostile to God's rule in our lives. *The law cannot change this hostility; it only further aggravates it.*

That's a big part of why God had to do something radically new in order to bring about our genuine obedience and spirituality.

INTO HIS ARMS

As believers, you and I have been delivered out of the arms of the law and into the arms of Christ. As Paul expresses it, you died to the law "that you may be married to another—to Him who was raised from the dead."

What a wondrous reality! Life is no longer to be lived under a code but through a Person, a breathtakingly glorious Person who is not only the unrivaled Sovereign of the universe but also the supreme Lover of our souls, One who infuses us moment by moment with resurrection power.

God's foremost calling for your life is a passionate and deepening love affair with His Son. When this is in place, God's standards will take care of themselves.

By contrast, being married to the law inevitably leads to despair. It's like living with Mr. Perfect. He never makes a mistake, never has a bad day, never indulges himself; he's always on time and on target in everything he does. Beyond this, he expects exactly the same from you. Perfection is your only acceptable standard, and he lets you know it every time you fail to measure up. If you do nine out of ten things right, you're still a failure.

Moreover, if you dare ask for his help in accomplishing the lists of responsibilities he keeps handing you, he turns a cold shoulder and tells you to try harder. It's all up to you. You feel an abiding sense of hopelessness.

How blessedly different is life married to our Lord! Instead of acceptance conditioned wholly by your performance, He assures you that you can never lose His love and provides you with an eternally significant purpose for living. He actually delights in you, and though He's displeased when you sin, this can never, ever cause Him to reject you. He sympathizes with your weaknesses and picks you up when you fall. Anything He asks you to do for Him, He Himself fully intends to do through you.

As Blaise Pascal expressed it, "The law demands what it cannot give; grace gives all it demands." No longer are we governed externally by a list of moral duties; we're now compelled internally to a lifestyle of radical, holy love because of the Person who's taken up residence within.

Of course many of the things your new Husband requires of you are the same things your former husband (the law) required, but now you do them freely, gladly, and even better than before. Grace always motivates and enables far beyond what law can do.

THE DESIRE IS THERE

Under the law, God's commands were *externally imposed*—written on tablets of stone and given to Israel with the requirement for wholehearted obedience. God's people were instructed with the repeated words, "You shall…" and "You shall not…"

But in the New Covenant, God's commands are now *internally implanted*—inscribed within us, just as God promised through His prophets: "I will put My law in their minds, and write it on their hearts." The watchword is no longer "You shall," but God's "I will": "*I will* put My law in their minds…and *I will* be their God…. *I will* forgive their iniquity"; "*I will* cleanse you…. *I will* give you a new heart…. *I will* put My Spirit within you and cause you to walk in My statutes."

What this startling truth means practically is that at the moment of your rebirth, God gave you a new set of godly inclinations, a divinely implanted disposition that always delights in doing His will. There is within you a Spirit-wrought disposition toward righteousness that can never be extinguished or diluted, though it can be submerged beneath other competing passions. *Within every believer, the desire to do the will of God is the gift of God.* This desire is not something to try and conjure up, but something already there, needing only to be nourished and appropriated.

This desire is there because the Holy Spirit now dwells in every believer. Normative Christianity is a blatantly supernatural affair, a life utterly dependent upon indwelling resurrection power from beginning to end. *The Old Covenant is man demonstrating what he can do for God; the New Covenant is God demonstrating what He can do for and through man.*

We could further define it in this way: The New Covenant is a radically different and radically better arrangement between God and His people, one that allows Him to accomplish in and through us what we're fundamentally incapable of doing under the law. It is God's "I will" overcoming our own "I can't."

Obedience New and True

While we're free from the law in the New Covenant, we are not free from obedience. Paul alluringly pictures this obedience in surprising ways.

He likens it, for example, to childbearing. You're married to Christ "that [you] should bear fruit to God" (fruit is often a metaphor for children in Scripture). What an enticing portrait! Our obedience is simply the by-product of being impregnated with Christ, the tangible evidence of the divinely implanted life within us.

True obedience is not gritting our teeth and "doing the right thing"; it is cooperating with the breaking forth of Christ's life from within. This fruit we bear as "children" to Christ includes not only new converts but also our godly character, good works, and worship.

Another image from Paul of our obedience is that of serving— "we should serve in the newness [freshness] of the Spirit and not in the oldness of the letter [the law]." There is service for God that seems musty-smelling, drab, lifeless. That's Old Covenant serving. But there's also a kind of ministry that has a fresh scent about it, one that exudes life and vitality. This is New Covenant serving, and with it "the fragrance of Christ" and "the aroma of life" are unmistakably present.

Awaiting Release

The writer of Hebrews salutes the New Covenant as "a better covenant" than the law because it is "established on better promises" and brings in "a better hope." Even so, it's amazing to see how quickly we gravitate back to the old.

We see this in popular approaches to spiritual maturity among the Christian community today. In his book *Connecting,* Larry Crabb identifies a couple of these.

The first he calls the *"Do what is right"* approach. This is the moralistic model and insists that people simply need to be exhorted to do what the Bible says. Change comes as people repent—turning away from the wrong and doggedly pursuing the right. Particularly among fundamental, conservative evangelicals, this course is widely followed. At its core, it's an Old Covenant attempt at sanctification. (*Sanctification* refers to how we live out the Christian life in a holy, godly way.)

The second approach he describes as *"Fix what is wrong."* This is the therapeutic model, which says people can't do what's right until damage from the past is looked at and healed. Change comes as people are repaired, namely by getting in touch with what's going on inside of them, facing their pain and disappointments, and courageously moving forward. Doing this requires help not provided by the gospel.

Clearly there are elements of truth in both models, for the gospel calls us to both do what is right and fix what is wrong. In both these systems, however, the means for change overlooks or denies the spiritual realities of the New Covenant in the life of the believer.

I would add yet another popular approach to this list, which could be called *"Get what is missing."* This is the power encounter model. It continually seeks miraculous experiences with God as the key to spiritual growth. Again there's clearly an element of truth here. We're indeed called to seek all God has for us and to mightily pursue His best. But how do we define God's best? A faith that requires an ongoing diet of signs and wonders will never mature properly.

A better model is what Larry Crabb calls *"Release what is good."* This is the very heartbeat of New Covenant spirituality. Because of the New Covenant, there are supernatural resources permanently residing within the soul of every believer, and they're the source of all spiritual good. Whatever "good" God wants to channel through us has *already* been placed within us; it simply awaits release.

This is what Jesus was alluding to when He promised, "He who believes in Me, as the Scripture has said, out of his heart will flow rivers of living water." We're to allow the good (living water) to be released in a constant flow.

Out of Hiding

Charles Spurgeon tells the story of a minister in the north of England who felt led to give a sizable sum to a very poor woman in his congregation. He took the money and went to her house. He knocked several times at her door; there was no answer.

Later he met her at church and told her he had come by.

"When?" she asked.

After he told her the time of his visit, she confessed she actually had been home; she thought he was a bill collector, and having no means to pay, she hid in her room. It was the pastor's joy to let the woman know his visit was to give her money, not take it away.

Many Christians respond to God in just the same fashion. They see Him mainly as the moral bill collector of the universe, knocking on the door of their life to demand the obedience that is due Him. Yet they sense within themselves such limited resources that they despair of ever being able to comply with His commands. Overwhelmed by guilt and frustration, they eventually run away from His voice rather than toward it.

The truth is that God comes to us first to give and only afterward to receive. Certainly He requires of us a lifestyle that honors His name; our obedience is His rightful due. But He never requires anything *from* us that He hasn't already deposited *within* us.

Let me say it again: *God requires from us only what He has already placed within us.*

We're called to let His living waters flow, to release what is good. This "good" is the full assortment of supernatural resources that were permanently implanted within you the instant you were born again and that are ready for release every day of your life on earth. In the heart of this book we'll explore in depth the four primary New Covenant provisions. My prayer is that as you discover more about them, releasing them will become easier indeed.

But to best understand and prepare for the most effective release of these provisions, we'll look first at their highest purpose, one that may be a surprise to you. Then we'll take a short but essential journey into a darkness that's absolutely necessary for gratefully and passionately appreciating the bright lights of the New Covenant.

Meanwhile, let me first invite you to pause and carefully consider your own life. Are you sensing a genuine hunger for greater freedom and the release of greater spiritual power? How open are you to the possibility that, at least in some ways, you may be hindered by an unrecognized law-based or legalistic approach to spirituality? Finally, let me encourage you throughout this book to biblically test and explore these principles for yourself. For this chapter, you might begin by prayerfully reading and meditating on 2 Corinthians 3, Romans 7, or Hebrews 8.

CHAPTER 2

First Things First: A Reputation at Stake

Put first things first and we get second things thrown in:
put second things first and we lose both first and second things.

C. S. LEWIS

As our new church building was being constructed I observed an interesting phenomenon. Everything built first—the support for all else to come—disappeared from sight long before the project was completed. The foundation I'd seen being poured into place, the huge steel girders I'd watched being erected above that—all this was eventually hidden by things like walls and windows and floors and ceilings.

Of course I knew this would happen. In fact I was impatient for such progress, eager to see the building's more practical aspects installed—the features we would keep on seeing and touching and using after moving in.

But what if the construction workers had skimped on those beginnings? Suppose they'd rushed too quickly through the substructure stages to get to the "good" stuff that's more visible and practical? The answer is that the building, if standing at all, would be unstable and unsafe.

I believe the same is true in constructing our best understanding of a life in Christ that soars like an eagle. Getting to the "good" stuff—the practical teaching we can most easily see and touch and use—requires first the right foundation of good theology.

That's why it's time in our fresh look at supernatural living to set a solid biblical foundation. If we're to make the radical adjustments required by New Covenant spirituality, we have to be absolutely convinced that these changes are called for by nothing less than the Word of God. "First things first" is as trustworthy an approach here as anywhere.

IS GOD ON YOUR SIDE?

So what exactly is "first" from God's viewpoint, according to His Word? What matters most to Him? What cause or issue is He most passionate about?

Early in America's Civil War a supporter of President Abraham Lincoln said he hoped the Lord was on the side of the North. Lincoln responded, "I know the Lord is always on the side of right. But," he added, "it is my constant anxiety and prayer that both myself and this nation should be on the Lord's side."

That exchange illustrates much of what ails the modern church. More often than not, Christianity today is marketed to the church and to the world as the best way to get the good Lord on your side, the sure path to getting the finest help available—namely God's. A casual look around the average Christian bookstore reveals a sizable percentage of books that basically focus on how to *use* God. Their message is clear and predictable: God is absolutely essential for making your life work. For success in finances, family, health, holiness, politics, and personal fulfillment, your approach must include God and His principles.

But a deeper reality seems all but forgotten: The main point of our spirituality, according to the Bible, is the *furthering of God's glory*, not the fixing of our lives. In other words, *God does not exist for us; we exist for Him.*

So the question isn't whether God is on our side, responsive to our call, but whether we are genuinely on His side, responsive to His call. It isn't how God fits into what we're doing, but how we fit into what He is doing. He is the Creator, we are the creatures. He is the Sovereign, we are the subjects. He is the Master, we are the slaves. He runs the universe, we fit in.

Sin, however, has introduced the insane proposition that we can alter or even reverse these roles. If God cannot be dismissed, at least He can be utilized. The bumper-sticker slogan speaks for many: "God Is My Copilot." We supposedly honor God by extending to Him a place in the cockpit of our lives, inviting His input on how we can fly smoothly and successfully through life, and of course turning to Him in any emergency cases. But the true and living God is no one's copilot. He's in absolute and sole control of where we're headed and solicits no one's advice on how to get there. In each of our lives, He relentlessly pushes forward His own kingdom agenda to its inevitable, glorious conclusion.

WHAT MATTERS MOST

From Genesis to Revelation we discover that God has one central purpose for creation and humankind. This is stated in various ways, but it all comes down to one main issue—His glory.

Nothing—*nothing*—matters more to God than the glory of His name. He is ablaze with a perfect, pure jealousy for His reputation. He told Moses,

> By those who come near Me
> I must be regarded as holy;
> And before all the people
> *I must be glorified.*

In the reckoning of God, failure to acknowledge His glory constitutes a capital offense, not the mere misdemeanor we would prefer to make it. Paul showed in the opening chapter of Romans that the ultimate reason for God's wrath against sinful mankind was that "they did not glorify Him as God." Because of failure to glorify God, Moses missed the Promised Land, Aaron's two oldest sons were killed, Nebuchadnezzar was made to live like an animal, Herod was eaten by worms…and so it goes throughout Scripture. One simply cannot escape the white-hot jealousy God has for His name and His glory.

Even our salvation has more to do with the acclaim it brings to God than the good it brings to us. When Paul speaks so upliftingly in Ephesians 1 of our salvation in Christ, he repeatedly points us to the purpose behind it—"to the praise of His glory." The most significant thing about your salvation and mine is the adoration and honor it brings to God.

In the same way, our ministry is important not primarily for how it blesses others, but for the recognition and renown it brings to God. Peter tells us we're to use our gifts in ministry to one another so that "in all things *God may be glorified* through Jesus Christ, to whom belong the glory and the dominion forever and ever. Amen."

"*Whatever* you do," Scripture says, "do all *to the glory of God.*" Our lives—together in the body of Christ as well as individually— must find their first and greatest significance in how they enhance God's reputation. This is our primary calling, the very purpose for our existence.

HEAVY AND SPECTACULAR

So what exactly is this "glory" of God?

I like to call it His "spectacularness." His glory is His stunning radiance, the overwhelming splendor of His excellence, His incomparable and exquisite beauty. The Hebrew term for "glory" comes from a root meaning "heavy" or "weighty." God's *glory* carries the full weight of all His attributes. The Bible likens that glory to images such as blinding light, raging fire, crashing thunder, flashing lightning, and a magnificent rainbow. Whatever else it may be, one thing is for sure—God's glory is awesome in appearance. It's too spectacular a sight to pass by without taking notice.

And He *wants* everyone to notice.

God's reputation has always been the whole point of human history and His foremost objective in choosing and blessing a people of His own. Through the prophet Isaiah we hear His voice calling out to "everyone who is called by My name, whom I have created *for My glory*"; we hear Him insisting, "This people I have formed for Myself; *they shall declare My praise.*" Responding in prayer, Isaiah acknowledges, "You lead Your people, to make Yourself *a glorious name.*"

God's utmost purpose for Israel was that they should spread His fame to surrounding nations. As the people of God lived out the commands of God, other nations would see His character fleshed out before them through acts of mercy, justice, and right-eousness. Israel's visible lifestyle would spotlight the invisible yet mighty God who reigned over them and over the universe. In that small strip of land called Israel, the Lord would make clear on earth what has always been known in heaven—that He alone is God and is more than worthy of people abandoning themselves to Him in joyous worship and service.

At Mount Sinai the Lord told His people, "You shall be to Me a kingdom of priests and a holy nation." As priests their role was to reflect God and dispense His Word to the rest of the world. As a holy nation, their character was in focus; they were to live as a "set apart" people, provoking those around them to seriously consider God as never before.

The Lord of heaven and earth was staking His reputation on the conduct of His children. Flesh-and-blood Israelites would serve as God's credentials, living proof that He alone is Lord. The spec-tacularness of God, the striking grandeur of God, would be seen through the most unlikely material of all—frail, faltering human-ity. This is the essential meaning of what it is to glorify God.

STILL AT STAKE

As we move into the New Testament we find striking parallels between Israel's calling and our own as members of Christ's body. In fact, using imagery virtually identical to God's words at Sinai, Peter tells us, "You are a chosen generation, a royal priesthood, a holy nation, His own special people, *that you may proclaim the praises of Him* who called you out of darkness into His marvelous light."

Once again God is staking His reputation on flesh and blood. As today's unbelievers observe God's children living in radical holiness, in supernatural community, and in overflowing grace, they too will be provoked to consider Christ in ways that a thousand tracts could never do.

Early in 1871, a worldly, roving journalist named Henry Stanley headed into Africa's uncharted interior to find Dr. David Livingstone, the famous explorer and medical missionary who for years had been cut off from contact with Europeans. Upon finding Livingstone ten months later, Stanley would go on to find something more, as he himself recounted:

> I went to Africa as prejudiced as the biggest atheist in
> London. But there came for me a long time of reflection. I
> saw this solitary old man there and asked myself, "How on
> earth does he stop here—is he cracked, or what? What
> inspires him?" For months after we met I found myself won-
> dering at the old man carrying out all that was said in the
> Bible—"Leave all things and follow Me." But little by little
> his sympathy for others became contagious, my sympathy
> was aroused; seeing his piety, his gentleness, his zeal, his
> earnestness, and how he went about his business, I was con-
> verted by him, although he had not tried to do it.

Later Stanley wrote, "It wasn't Livingstone's preaching that converted me, it was his living."

This is what it means to serve as Christ's credentials: We live in such a way that people around us become intrigued with the reason behind it.

"The first duty of the Christian," wrote John Calvin, "is to make the invisible kingdom visible." This can happen only when the divine resources of the New Covenant are unleashed in our lives.

WHERE GOD WAS BURIED

Unfortunately the Israelites failed tragically in their calling. Instead of glorifying His name—His character, His reputation, His authority—they did just the opposite. Through the prophet Ezekiel, God pronounced His indictment against them: "They profaned My holy name."

The Hebrew word translated as "profane" basically means "to treat as common or ordinary." Their lives had made God "ordinary." They had neutered God's reputation on earth. There was nothing in their conduct that elevated the name of their God over that of the many run-of-the-mill gods of their day. Certainly the Israelites claimed that He was the only true God, but nothing in their lifestyle required this claim be taken seriously.

That Hebrew word for "profane" can also be translated "to wound." In a real sense Israel wounded God's prestige; His name now limped among the nations.

How did Israel do this?

Speaking again through Ezekiel, God gave the answer: "I poured out My fury on them *for the blood they had shed* on the land, and *for their idols* with which they had defiled it." Their land was stained by *idolatry* and by *bloodshed*. God's two greatest commands for His people—to fully love God and to love one's neighbor as one's self—were being flagrantly violated.

Rather than giving God their undivided trust and adoration, Israel turned to the idols of the nations around them. And so they communicated a blatant message to all those around: "God is not trustworthy enough or powerful enough to stake our lives upon. He doesn't come through. He just can't get the job done."

In addition to their idolatry, God's people resorted to unrestrained selfishness instead of relating to one another in a way that reflected God's justice and love. Rampant hatred, to the point of bloodshed, replaced godly concern for one another.

They were no longer God's showcase. Instead, Israel in a sense had become His burial ground, for nothing about them gave convincing proof that the God who parted the Red Sea was still alive.

The land of Israel had become like a beautiful wall spray-painted with ugly graffiti that blared two central messages: *God can't be trusted* and *People don't matter.*

IS GOD ENOUGH?

Is the same message blaring from God's people today?

The local church is where God is seeking to go public—not just a place where the gospel's truth is talked about, but where the gospel's attractiveness is visible. The local church, as Francis Schaeffer said, "should be right, but it should also be beautiful." It's through the community of Spirit-inhabited saints, more than any other way, that God intends to show the darkened world the kind of God He is.

Therefore two chief callings rest upon us. The first is to live in such a way that our lives boldly proclaim, "There is only one God worthy of undivided trust and unrestrained adoration." The Bible calls this *faith.*

The second calling is to care for one another in such a way that unbelievers are amazed. The Scriptures call this *love.*

This combination is what puts God on display most noticeably before the world—our radical dependency in an unseen God plus our extraordinary concern for other people (especially fellow believers). Paul calls it "faith working through love."

Yet, like the Israelites of old, we can "defile the land." When we let other gods (money, career, approval, achievement, possessions, pornography, or whatever) meet our needs, we proclaim to all those around, "God is not enough." And when we treat one another with indifference or disdain, when legalistic standards matter more than fellow saints, when church is more like a corporation than a family, we communicate to the world that people don't matter all that much.

Sheldon Vanauken captures a paradox:

> The best argument for Christianity is Christians; their joy, their certainty, their completeness. But the strongest argument against Christianity is also Christians—when they are somber and joyless, when they are narrow and repressive, then Christianity dies a thousand deaths.

The great tragedy and heinousness of our sin is not primarily the destruction it brings to our lives but the crippling it brings to God's name. Whenever a believer sins—whether it be the godless hedonism of license or the cold hardness of legalism—the worst result is that the glory of God is for that moment obscured; His name is made to limp. When our conduct nullifies our profession of God's greatness, when our lives fail to reflect the presence of resurrection power, we profane God's name.

TO THE RESCUE

In the same passage from the prophet Ezekiel where God charged Israel with profaning His name and defiling the land, He confirmed also that He "had concern" for His holy name. The Hebrew word here means "to take pity upon" or "to have compassion toward." The same word is used of Pharaoh's daughter having "compassion" when she found the baby Moses floating in a basket in the river, a compassion that caused her to rescue the child. As God saw His name lying wounded in Israel, He was stirred deeply to rescue it from further abuse.

How would He do it?

In this same chapter of Ezekiel, God sheds light on His promise of a New Covenant. "I will take you," He said.

> I will cleanse you from all your filthiness and from all your idols. I will give you a new heart and put a new spirit within you; I will take the heart of stone out of your flesh and give you a heart of flesh. I will put My Spirit within you and cause you to walk in My statutes.

In later chapters, we'll delve deeply into these incredible promises. But for now, consider *why* God was making them. "I do not do this," God said through Ezekiel, "for your sake, O house of Israel, *but for My holy name's sake,* which you have profaned." What spurred Him on to divine intervention was not the rescue of His people, *but the rescue of His name!*

God's controlling passion, His supreme concern, His unflinching priority is the grandeur and splendor of who He is. His matchless name may be scorned by the proud, blurred by those misrepresenting it, and yawned at by fools; but sooner or later God will come to its rescue.

And that rescue *will* succeed.

God is not merely hoping or wishing that someday we will give Him His rightful due. He is ensuring it by active pursuit, steering all history toward that day when every knee will bow and every tongue confess "that Jesus Christ is Lord, *to the glory of God the Father.*" In His own timing and by His own means He will continue to set high over all peoples and nations that infinite glory belonging to His name alone. Already, this very moment, He is harvesting His glory from among the nations through the spread of His gospel and the worship and testimony of His people.

To be sure, the global conquest of God's glory will not fully occur until Christ Himself personally returns to set up His kingdom. In the meantime, you and I are part of a community whose central purpose is to participate with God in His relentless march toward seeing His name rightly exalted.

SURPRISED? OFFENDED?

All this is *not* to say that people don't matter to God. He created us, He pursues us, He provides for us, He even died for us. The whole of Scripture testifies to the wondrous reality of His unfathomable love toward us. *We matter much to God…but we don't matter most.* We can't and we shouldn't.

You see, an infinitely perfect God must supremely value that which *is* of supreme value. If He doesn't, He's no longer perfect. If God were to value people over His name, the inversion would disqualify Him from being God.

Yet so many Christians are surprised or even offended to be told that what counts most to God is His glory, not us. Many of us have grown up all our lives hearing that *we* rank first to God, because of His love. But this cannot be true, as we'll continue to discover in very practical terms. And precisely because it isn't true, our highest well-being is assured.

C. S. Lewis was right: "Put first things first and we get second things thrown in: put second things first and we lose both first and second things." When God is approached primarily as the great

Fixer of life, with *our* needs as His prime agenda, our lives will not only fail to reflect His glory, but we'll also fail to experience change and fulfillment in the deepest, richest sense. However, when we delight most in the spectacularness of God, when His glory becomes our highest agenda, we find a taste that thrills our souls plus we experience a nonstop transformation in our lives along the way.

In light of the issues raised in this chapter, how might you have viewed God inadequately? That's a good question to think about as you look at Ephesians 1, Colossians 1, or 1 Peter 2.

Becoming Spiritually Provocative

Preach the gospel at all times. If necessary, use words.

F R A N C I S   O F   A S S I S I

I have a pair of sunglasses I especially like. I don't know exactly what kind of special tinting the lenses have, but it sure changes the way everything looks. Greens are greener, yellows are brighter—every color seems a bit more vivid. In fact, I hate to take them off.

When the glory of God takes possession of us, it's very much like wearing those sunglasses. Everything looks different! There's a new vividness to life, a heightening of purpose, a clarity of focus, and a vibrancy of spirit that belong only to those held captive by His glory. Moreover, we'll joyously embrace God's goal for our lives to make us not just spiritually *whole* but spiritually *provocative.*

God's highest agenda for our lives is not that they be simply good, moral, and responsible, but that they be spiritually intriguing, even mystifying. God wants us "conformed to the image of His Son," as Paul says, and a Christlike life is one that puzzles, attracts, disrupts, entices, enrages, comforts, rebukes, and most of all, radically loves those around it. It's a life that will provoke others to a new contemplation of God.

So the central issue is not what kind of obedience will prompt God to make our life more manageable and successful, but what kind of obedience will make God's excellence more visible on the playing field of life. What *specifically* does such obedience look like for you and for me?

UNIQUE APPLICATIONS

When John the Baptist was preaching in the wilderness to huge crowds about repentance, the crowds asked him, "What shall we do?"

John could have answered with a generalized "Love God and do what is right." But he was much more specific: "He who has two tunics, let him give to him who has none; and he who has food, let him do likewise."

This challenging answer was designed to promote both *radical trust in an unseen God* and *genuine concern for others' needs*. As the people gave away their extra to those in need, they demonstrated that their trust was not in any surplus but in a faithful God. In giving to those in need, they reflected a God-like concern for others.

John was later approached by a group of tax collectors and then by a band of soldiers—two sets of people quite different from each other and from the crowd at large. Like the larger crowd, both the tax collectors and the soldiers asked John separately, "What shall we do?"

Again John could have responded with a generic answer, or at least the same response he gave earlier. Instead he carefully crafted applications that were unique to each group. Why did he do so? Because each group had a distinctive sphere of influence and therefore its own opportunity *to unleash the glory of God* in that sphere.

He told the tax collectors, "Collect no more than what is appointed for you." He answered the soldiers, "Do not intimidate anyone or accuse falsely, and be content with your wages." He asked both groups to do what was almost unheard of in that day. (Tax collectors who taxed fairly and soldiers who didn't bully or bribe would get everybody's attention.)

Three groups…three separate answers. In each case the questioners were to approach life in a radically different manner than what was normal, enabling them to shake up people's perspectives on God.

The bottom line: *Give others a clearer glimpse of God.*

What Shall We Do?

That's also the bottom line for us.

Do we see our work primarily as a place to earn a paycheck or advance our career? Paul taught workers in their labor to "adorn the doctrine of God our Savior in all things." With a view to that kind of "adornment"—God's glory—we learn to see the marketplace first and foremost as an arena for displaying the light of the gospel.

How do we respond to authority? Do we show respect and submission mainly because it keeps us out of trouble? When our aim is to glorify God, true respect and submission signals to the world our confidence in One who's infinitely greater than any human authority. Peter says this is one of the ways unbelievers will be impacted so that they "glorify God in the day of visitation"— the day God draws near to them.

How about marriage? As a husband and wife learn to glorify God and allow themselves to be Spirit-dominated, they see their relationship not as a filling station for their own needs but a way to clearly reflect resurrection power. When their needs are unmet by one another, they're able to view it not as a blockade to happiness but as an opportunity for supernatural responding, thereby increasing glory for God.

And our prayer life? When God's name and interests are paramount, our prayer is not, "Our Father who art in heaven, please bankroll the needs I'm about to tell You," but rather, "Hallowed be Your name. Your kingdom come. Your will be done on earth as it is in heaven." His name and His kingdom receive top billing in our petitions, before we move to personal needs.

FOR OUR CHILDREN

Perhaps you're a parent. What will a focus on God's glory mean for you in that arena?

The prophet Malachi tells us that the Lord "seeks godly offspring" from our marriages. His design for our children (as for all of us) is that they be not merely well-adjusted, contributing members of society, but living dispensers of His spectacularness wherever He stations them on this earth.

As I consider my three sons, this perspective has tremendous ramifications. When I think about them, pray for them, and relate to them, I must do so transcendently. I must realize there's something at stake in their lives far greater than their own well-being and comfort, something that surpasses all the pleasures and heartaches earth has to offer.

What do I want for them? Is it good grades, a good college, a satisfying job, a good marriage, a good family, involvement in a good church, and finally a secure retirement? Certainly I would enjoy seeing these things for each of my sons. But viewing them through the lens of God's glory requires me to see something greater.

What I want most is that they "max out" (to use their lingo) all their unique potential for advancing God's reputation. These three men are "His workmanship, created in Christ Jesus for good works, which God prepared beforehand." Whatever these preordained works are, whatever God's distinctive design is for each of my sons, it all centers on making His excellence known. What matters most is that they discover and participate in their God-crafted niche for shining forth His glory in this dark world. This alone will determine their true success.

Such a perspective has been critical for me in being able to deal with their disabilities. Two of my sons have significant learning disabilities; one is mildly affected by cerebral palsy. As I father them, I've been ministered to time and again by C. S. Lewis's statement, "Every disability conceals a vocation." It reminds me that God has an eternally significant purpose behind their disabilities, a distinct vocation for glorifying Him, something that transcends any other achievement.

This vocation may mean going to college…but it may not. At times it may mean a comfortable, secure job; it might also mean getting fired. It may mean a happy, fulfilling marriage, but there's no guarantee. It may mean raising their own children who love and serve God, or they may live with the heartache of a prodigal. The all-important issue is that, whatever circumstances God places them in, their lives are to display His spectacularness through their own unique design.

My parenting must be much more concerned with helping them hear and respond to God's call than simply getting them to conform to my standards of behavior. I must have big enough dreams and aspirations for them, dreams that go beyond happy, successful, respectable lives. If I can be used of the Spirit to help each one move toward his God-crafted niche and be increasingly caught up in the Lord's glory, I will have given them the greatest gift fatherhood has to offer.

TWO TRAINS

So we see that there are fundamentally two ways to approach our spiritual lives: live for God so that we can fully exploit His blessings, or live for Him so He can fully reveal His name.

A few years ago my wife and I took a train from New York City to New Haven, Connecticut. As we boarded the train in Grand Central Station I noticed another train right beside ours, one whose posted destination was a city hundreds of miles from New Haven. Both trains headed out in the same direction. Yet the farther we went, the greater divergence there was between the two. What began as identical directions ended up being far, far apart.

A similar thing is happening today in the church. We're inviting people to board one of two trains for their spiritual journey.

The first is far and away the most popular. It says Christianity is primarily about God benefiting His creatures. This approach teaches that what matters most to God is people. Their well-being—spiritual, physical, and psychological—is what drives His actions and determines His priorities. Passengers on this train keep asking, "What must I do to gain God's blessing?"

"The church of North America has become so success oriented," said Eugene Nida, "that we go from seminar to seminar on how to use God, but few are sitting in quiet holiness asking, 'How can God use me?'"

The second approach is less popular but infinitely more biblical. It teaches that Christianity is primarily about God's glorifying His name. This is His core motivation for all He does. On this train, the passengers keep asking, "What can I do to better reflect God's glory?"

Early on, both these approaches look quite similar. But the farther one goes on life's journey, the more significant the difference becomes, especially in things like suffering, sacrifice, submission, prayer, and ministry.

SEE THE DIFFERENCE

What practical difference will it make if we focus first on God's glory?

The difference will show in our humility and personal brokenness.

Early in Isaiah, the prophet is pronouncing "woe" upon other people: "Woe to those who draw iniquity with cords of vanity.... Woe to those who call evil good, and good evil." But in the very next chapter he sees "the Lord sitting on a throne, high and lifted up." In the blinding light of God's blazing holiness, Isaiah's "woe" turns inward: "Woe is *me*," he cries, "for I am undone!" He now recognizes that he isn't all that different from those he has just been condemning.

The air in a room appears clear until a sunbeam enters through a window. Then, in the light of that ray, you see countless particles of dust for the first time. In the same way, the depths of our sin remain hidden until seen in the light of God's holy excellence.

Truly confronting God's glory will also ignite a holy zeal within us for His name, as it did for young David when he shouted to Goliath, "I come to you *in the name of the LORD of hosts,* the God of the armies of Israel, whom you have defied."

Years later, the Son of David would do battle with the religious establishment of His day by making a whip and driving out "money-changers" from the temple, overturning their tables and scattering their coins. What drove Jesus to such lengths? At the time, these actions caused His disciples to remember a prophecy in Scripture: "Zeal for Your house has eaten Me up." It was fiery zeal for His Father's reputation that brought this astonishing outburst from Jesus.

Being absorbed with God's glory will also result in the purifying of our lives—so that we're "transformed," as Paul says, "from glory to glory." We can't transform ourselves, but God's Spirit accomplishes it, Paul explains, while we're "beholding as in a mirror the glory of the Lord." To be transformed, our job is to "behold"—to continually contemplate—God's glory, focusing our spiritual gaze not primarily on things like Christian duties or our unworthiness, but on God's spectacularness.

INGODDED PEOPLE

Nothing so invigorates our souls, so ravishes our hearts, so diminishes our anxieties, and so ennobles our existence as being supremely preoccupied with God's greatness and presence. This is what you and I were made for.

That's why glorifying God and satisfying ourselves is a win-win proposition. In fact, as John Piper explained it, God's deepest commitment (to His glory) and our own deepest longing "are not in conflict, but...find simultaneous consummation" when we glorify God. This is what Piper called "the wonder of the gospel" and the most freeing discovery he'd ever made.

But this supernatural outcome requires the unleashing of supernatural resources. For others to notice God in His people, there must be literally something of *Him* inside of us. That's why God, in the New Covenant, made His promise to invade and indwell us, creating a whole new society of "ingodded" (to use Dante's term) men and women.

This is as it must be—for our flesh is wholly incapable of pulling off the divine performance for which God has prepared us. It takes nothing less than indwelling deity to override sin's power and display handiwork worthy of God's name. And nothing less is what God indeed has provided.

I encourage you to ask yourself, What does focusing first on God's glory look like in my work, in how I relate to those in authority over me, in my marriage and family, and in my prayers? And take a look when you can at God's dealings with His people in Ezekiel 36.

CHAPTER 4

The Journey to Radical Dependence

What terrifies us is not the explosive force of the atomic bomb,
but the power of the wickedness of the human heart.

ALBERT EINSTEIN

Years ago the children of a family vacationing on the Gulf Coast in Texas came across a soaked and scraggly little dog. Unable to find its owner, they prevailed upon their parents to take it home with them.

Back home, they washed and groomed their new pet. The next morning they left it alone in the house with food, water, and their pet cat. Returning later in the day, they discovered that their cat was deceased. Badly deceased in fact. It was also clear that their new pet was the culprit.

The following day the parents took the dog to the vet, thinking it wise to have it checked out. The vet informed them that the creature they'd taken in wasn't really a dog at all—it was an African rat. Apparently it had found its way ashore from an oceangoing ship docked along the coast.

A rat is a rat is a rat. It doesn't matter whether it's cleaned and groomed or dirty and scraggly, whether it lives in a sewer or a palace, whether it's cared for or shunned. Wherever it lives, whatever it looks like, however it smells, it will always be a rat.

The same is equally true concerning what the Bible calls our "flesh," that God-hostile, self-centered part of us often referred to as our "fallen nature" or "sin nature" or "carnal nature." Whether our flesh hangs out in church or at a bar, whether it's highly disciplined or self-indulgent, whether it's intoxicated by religious success or by alcoholic drink, it is still flesh. No matter how respectable it looks, how refined its manners, how religious its conduct, its fundamental nature remains unaltered. It is sin-riddled through and through, with no hope whatsoever of improvement.

That's why Jesus told his disciples, "The flesh profits nothing." Notice He didn't say "little." The word is *nothing*. No amount of self-help, positive thinking, therapy, meditation, or discipline will ever improve this nature. It is flesh, will always be flesh, and will always have absolutely nothing to offer our spirituality.

We really don't believe this, however, and that could be our main problem as Christians.

The Beginning of God

If I were in the room with you now and tried handing you a life jacket, you probably would turn it down. At best you might politely hold it before setting it aside once I'd left.

If however we were on a sinking ship in the middle of the ocean, you would take hold of that same life jacket with a passion.

We're born into this world on a sinking ship, wholly enslaved to sin. God holds out a life jacket—the provisions of the New

Covenant. But until we're convinced that our plight is truly desperate, we won't seize hold of God's offer.

Of course this is true first of all in our need to come to Christ for salvation. But after we're saved and continuing on in the Christian life, how many of us essentially take off the life jacket and try swimming again on our own?

Even as Christians, we won't flee to the supernatural resources provided only by God until all hope and confidence in our natural resources is shattered. "The end of ourselves," as someone put it, "is the beginning of God."

This chapter's journey into darkness is not a pleasant one, but it's absolutely essential. By better understanding our inner devastation, we'll more quickly turn to a radical dependence upon God and His supernatural enablement.

Such a Heart

Many decades ago a columnist in the London *Times* often ended his articles with the words, "What's wrong with the world?" According to a commonly told story, G. K. Chesterton finally sent in the following response.

> Dear Editor:
>
> What's wrong with the world? I am.
>
> Faithfully yours,
> G. K. Chesterton

Chesterton understood the Bible's teaching on humanity's central problem: It's *us;* more specifically, it's what lies *in* us.

At Mount Sinai, when Moses was receiving the law from God, the people confidently told him, "Tell us all that the LORD our God says to you, and we will hear and do it." There's no hint here of insincerity; they were fully resolved to do God's will—all of it. (How often have you and I done the same? We clearly hear the convicting voice of God in church, or at a retreat, or in a moment of quiet prayer…and with highest hopes and best intentions we promise that *we* will now make our lives different.)

Hearing the people's words, God responded, "Oh, that they had *such a heart* in them that they would fear Me and always keep all My commandments." He knew that the kind of "heart" necessary to obey Him was missing in every one of them, as they themselves would quickly and tragically demonstrate.

Forty years later, as the people prepared to finally enter the Promised Land, God gave them their first promise of the New Covenant: "The LORD your God will *circumcise your heart* and the heart of your descendants, to love the LORD your God *with all your heart.*"

MUD IN A SLUM

Heart is the word the Bible uses most often to describe the whole of our interior life. The heart is our "control central." In Scripture it refers to our intellect, to our emotions, to our will, and to our conscience.

Heart also refers to our spiritual yearnings. God has created us with deep cravings in our spirit especially for *relationship* and for *impact.* We hunger to be loved so relentlessly and unconditionally that we won't have to perform for acceptance. We also hunger to make an unerasable difference in our world, to leave an imprint from our lives that will never be washed away by the tide of time.

All five of these components of our heart—intellect, emotions, will, conscience, and spiritual longings—were created by God and are good in and of themselves. All five were to be used for glorifying Him. But all five have been badly warped because of the Fall.

Our mind was given to discover and ponder God's character and truth, but we've used it instead to produce and embrace poisonous philosophies and self-centered rationalizations. Our intellect has become "darkened," to use the New Testament word. We don't think as God thinks. Our thoughts have become so clouded by innate sinfulness that we're incapable of God-honoring rationality.

Our emotions were given for loving God and others, but they've been degraded, "serving various lusts and pleasures," as Paul says. We love what we should hate and hate what we should love.

Our will is God's wonderful gift for choosing and going in His direction, but it has become defiant instead. As Isaiah says, "We have turned, every one, to his own way."

The conscience is our internal alarm system from God, to warn us when moral danger is impending and to confirm when we're doing right. But our conscience has become defiled and is no longer reliable as a moral compass.

Finally, our spiritual appetites have become diverted to the point that Paul could say, "There is none who seeks after God." These desires have not been extinguished, but rather rerouted; we drink spiritually at muddy watering holes to quench our thirst and eat from the city dump to satisfy our hunger. C. S. Lewis pictured our situation as "an ignorant child who wants to go on making mud pies in a slum because he cannot imagine what is meant by the offer of a holiday by the sea."

Ultimately all sin is taking one of these God-given longings and going in a God-absent direction to fulfill them. George MacDonald was pointing to this when he made the daring assertion that when a man knocks at a brothel, he is really knocking for God.

In short, our hearts have become wholly infected by the cancer of sin. We're hopelessly short-circuited in our wiring for godly righteousness and joy.

Needless to say, this isn't our culture's prevailing view of ourselves. However, until we understand (as someone has observed) that in our fallen state we much more closely resemble Adolf Hitler than Jesus Christ, we don't yet grasp the Bible's take on humanity and sin.

ARE WE THAT BAD?

But, come on, is our natural heart really *that* bad? Obviously we're fallen, but aren't words like *warped, darkened, degraded,* and *defiled* a bit harsh and exaggerated to describe our inner natures? And what about all the seemingly good people who aren't Christians but who do so much to help others and to better the world—are they really wicked, warped, defiled?

The answer rests on our standard of measurement. The true standard for goodness and righteousness is given us by God. In fact, the standard *is* God. Without keeping this fact in focus, we remain naively optimistic concerning our own and others' moral capabilities.

We easily slip into a "street level" view of goodness. It's like walking down a city sidewalk and comparing the heights of those you pass by. A few people happen to be well over six feet tall and really stand out from the crowd. But if you were to look down on the same scene from atop a hundred-story skyscraper, everybody on the sidewalk would appear equally tiny.

When God looks down on all humanity from heaven, what's His assessment? The Bible speaks directly to this. "God looks down from heaven upon the children of men," David tells us, "to see if there are any who understand, who seek God." What does God find? "Every one of them has turned aside; they have together become corrupt; there is none who does good, no, not one."

Paul quoted that passage to the believers in Rome, introducing it with this sentence: "There is none righteous, no, not one." Those words focus on our *internal disposition* toward sin. We're all unrighteous sinners by *nature*. And David's words—"there is none who *does* good, no, not one"—focus on our *external actions* of sin. We're also sinners by *deed*. Our actions are tainted by the same dye of sin that permeates our fallen nature.

DRUNKEN PEASANTS

We see a similar dual aspect of sin throughout Scripture. Paul says we're to "cleanse ourselves from all filthiness of the *flesh* and *spirit*."

Sins of the flesh are things like drunkenness, fornication, and stealing that violate God's moral standards for external holiness. Sins of the spirit are things like pride, envy, and unforgiveness that violate His standards for internal holiness. This second category is as evil as the first, if not more so. Listen to C. S. Lewis again:

> The sins of the flesh are bad, but they are the least bad of all sins. All the worst pleasures are purely spiritual: the pleasure of putting other people in the wrong, of bossing and patronising and spoiling sport, and back-biting; the pleasures of

power, of hatred. For there are two things inside me, competing with the human self which I must try to become. They are the animal self, and the Diabolical self. The Diabolical self is the worse of the two. That is why a cold, self-righteous prig who goes regularly to church may be far nearer to hell than a prostitute. But, of course, it is better to be neither.

In the parable Jesus told about the prodigal son, the younger brother's misdeeds were sins of the flesh. Meanwhile the failures of his older brother were sins of the spirit. Why did Jesus make this older son out to be a bad guy? After all, here was the epitome of responsibility and obedience.

The answer strikes home when we look at the situation in which Jesus told this story. Luke sets the scene: "All the tax collectors and the sinners drew near to Him to hear Him. And the Pharisees and scribes complained, saying, 'This Man receives sinners and eats with them.'"

We find two quite distinct groups hanging around Jesus. First are the easily recognized sinners of the day, tax collectors and the like (comparable to today's pimps, prostitutes, and drug dealers). They *knew* they were sinners and had little interest in religiosity, but they found Jesus wonderfully alluring (just as today's blatant "sinners" often do).

The other group was the well-camouflaged sinners—Pharisees and scribes, society's religious leaders (like some of today's preachers, deacons, and Sunday-school teachers). They were thoroughly orthodox, doctrinally sound, and morally upright. They were also wholly unaware of their pervasive sinfulness.

In the story Jesus told on this occasion, the younger son—the "prodigal"—represented the tax collectors and sinners. Unencumbered by the restraints of religion and morality, their lives were characterized by wanton drinking and partying, cheating on taxes and on spouses, lying and stealing to get ahead. Here was *blatant disobedience* of God's standards—in other words, *sin*.

The older brother represented the Pharisees and scribes. Their lives were marked by slavish and joyless devotion to obedience and duty, by disciplined morality, grim piety, rigid law-keeping, smug superiority. Here was *counterfeit obedience* of God's standards—in other words, *sin*. They thought of unrighteousness only in terms of others' actions, such as lying or stealing, and missed the often greater unrighteousness of godless attitudes underlying their own "good" deeds.

In this vein, it's interesting to note the father's response to his older son's lack of inward righteousness. "Son," the father told him, "you are always with me, and all that I have is yours." In other words, "I myself, as well as all my provisions, are always with you; what more could you want?"

The same holds true for us all. Oswald Chambers wrote that the root of sin is unbelief in the goodness of God. Sin is every bit as much about distrust of God's heart and hand as it is about defiance of His standards. All sin ultimately makes its way back to our firmly rooted distrust of God and our desperate determination to find life on our own.

Martin Luther was exactly right: "The world resembles a drunken peasant; when you lift him into the saddle on one side, he tumbles off on the other." All of us topple to the side of either legalism or license. Our flesh erupts in either the younger son's blatant disobedience or the older son's counterfeit obedience. Personally, I know I've come to see more of that older brother in me than I ever cared to know.

What, Why, How

Does all this mean it's impossible for any unbeliever, or any Christian relying on his own effort, to do anything good or righteous?

Again, the answer depends on the standard of measurement. God views our deeds from three angles through what I like to call His "trifocals." He scrutinizes not only *what* we do, but also *why* we do it and *how.*

He measures *what* we do by His directives in Scripture. To violate those directives is clearly sin, yet meeting this standard is more difficult than most of us realize. Jesus summarized the whole of God's mandate by saying we're to unreservedly love God and to love our neighbor as ourselves. The standard is simply a life wholly abandoned to perfect loving! (This is why the litmus test for how we're doing spiritually is not the Ten Commandments, but 1 Corinthians 13.) To meet this standard requires that we spend every waking moment of our existence in loving God and others perfectly. Moreover, Christ gave this mandate an internal dimension, showing us by way of example that unresolved anger and hatred toward someone will incur judgment in God's eyes just as surely as murder will. According to Jesus, adultery can take place not only in bed but also in our heart.

Second, God measures *why* we do something—our motivation—by the biblical standard that everything be done for His glory. Drawing attention to God must be the central purpose behind all our actions. This is why Scripture says that to sin is to "fall short of the glory of God." If we avoid adultery only from fear of getting caught, or from not wanting to destroy our marriage, or from concern for our children, but without any concern for God's name, then that avoidance (commendable as it is!) doesn't qualify as "good" from God's perspective.

Finally, God measures *how* we do something by the biblical standard that everything be done in active and continual dependence on Christ ("abiding" in Him). For any of our deeds to qualify as "good" in God's eyes, He Himself must do it through us! This is why Jesus told us, "Without Me you can do nothing." We can be sincerely motivated to abstain from adultery for the sake of God's glory...but how do we accomplish it? Is it simply by gritting our teeth and walking away from temptation through sheer willpower? Or is there an underlying desperation that says, "Lord, apart from Your strength and indwelling purity I will surely fall; O God, please help me appropriate Your overcoming grace to walk away"?

Meeting God's standards on all three of these levels has been accomplished in history only by one life, and it isn't yours or mine. Only Jesus Christ always did all of the will of God, for the glory of God, through the power of God. Only the Lamb is worthy. This is why we need Him so desperately at every turn.

Spinach in Our Teeth

One of the most ratlike tendencies in all of us is that of judging one another. Yet judging is like throwing a boomerang. Paul says, "In whatever you judge another you condemn yourself; for you who judge practice the same things."

One evening my wife and I were washing dishes together when I noticed a fairly sizable piece of spinach caught in Sandy's teeth. It looked so funny I started laughing and somewhat gleefully pointed it out to her.

She looked at me and said, "You might want to check your own teeth."

Sure enough, my teeth sported a piece of spinach at least as big as the one in hers.

Spiritually speaking, we all have spinach in our teeth. From God's viewpoint, whenever we judge a sin in someone else's life, there's sure to be a similar kind of sin in ours if we look hard enough. We may not steal money like the thief we condemn, but how often in a typical day do we steal the glory that belongs only to God, or steal from someone's good name by talking behind her back?

It's easy to condemn those who are enslaved to alcohol or drugs. Normally their addiction has come about through peer pressure or seeking to escape reality. But how often do we join with the crowd or try to numb reality through addiction to sports, shopping, overeating, or whatever?

It seems to me that we fall into judgmentalism especially in the case of homosexuality. At its core, this sin is simply taking a legitimate longing (for love, acceptance, intimacy) and going in an illegitimate direction. Do we do this? Of course. It may be through illicit heterosexual activity or through what's often called codependency—relying on someone for what only God can provide—or through a variety of more socially acceptable means.

How easily and consistently we underrate our own sinful reality! "The human heart," John Calvin observed, "has so many recesses for vanity, so many lurking places for falsehood, is so shrouded by fraud and hypocrisy, that it often deceives itself."

Even our service for God is not exempt from the flesh's control. We might teach a Sunday-school class because of sensing a genuine call from God and joyfully responding in obedience. Or it might be no more than yielding feebly to someone's pressured phone call or our fear of looking bad if we didn't volunteer. Until we understand that the passion of the flesh that drives one person to take drugs may be the same passion that drives another to teach Sunday school, we haven't yet understood the Bible's teaching on sin.

GOD'S REMEDY

By honestly recognizing the standards an infinitely holy God must use, we can more readily agree that there's no one among us who's righteous, no one who does good—"no, not one."

A rat is a rat is a rat.

This is dismal news. But *God's intent in clearly exposing our sinfulness is not to make us feel bad.* It's to make us feel *desperate*—to shatter every vestige of confidence in ourselves. If we merely feel disheartened or discouraged by this chapter, our pride still remains intact at some level. Only after we lose all hope of attaining on our own what God requires will we stop relying on self and start passionately taking hold of what God has provided.

God's remedy to this deep trouble caused by our fallen nature is not an exhortation to try harder. Nor is it a program to help improve or upgrade our natural heart, since such progress is actually impossible.

No, God's solution is to offset our old heart with a new one— the "circumcised" heart He promised Israel at the border of the Promised Land. "I will give them a heart to know Me," God says through the prophet Jeremiah. "I will give you a new heart and put a new spirit within you," He adds through the prophet Ezekiel.

We'll discover that this new heart is exactly the opposite of the old. Rather than being cold and unyielding to God, inclined toward evil, and captivated by foolishness, this one is warmly animated toward God, inclined toward righteousness, and captivated by truth.

And it's wholly the gift of God; it can only be received, not developed.

In bestowing this gift at our conversion, God doesn't remove our old heart. When we trust Christ for salvation, our sinful nature is not *removed* but *offset*. Till the day we die there will always be a godless, proud, innately wicked part of us that will never be improved over time. Yet within every believer there will also be a godly, righteous, Christ-adoring inclination that can never be destroyed (although it can be stifled by other passions).

Which nature are we depending on?

Sometimes, by listening carefully to our thoughts, we'll recognize our lingering confidence in the flesh: *I guarantee things will be different from now on… I can't believe I did something that bad; it will never happen again… If only I had tried harder.*

But with a New Covenant approach we'll learn to face reality:

"My only hope for doing better from now on is to fall back on God's strength at every turn. Please Lord, help me do this."

"I'm frankly not too surprised I did that; when I'm not consciously depending on Christ's strength, I'm capable of doing far worse."

"No matter how hard I tried, it wouldn't have helped; I just wasn't really relying on the Lord at that moment."

As we prepare now to dive into discovering and appropriating God's New Covenant provisions, what evidence do you see in your own heart and life of lingering confidence in the flesh? To assist in this self-discovery, meditate on the first three chapters of Romans.

Releasing Your New Purity

We must take refuge from God in God.

A. W. TOZER

The Christian life isn't hard; it's flat-out impossible. It becomes possible only when God injects His fullness into His people's hearts—which is exactly what He's done in the New Covenant.

With this chapter we begin exploring the New Covenant's four primary spiritual provisions: your new *purity,* your new *identity,* your new *disposition,* and your new *power.* Each is purely the gift of God alone, received through Christ alone, by faith alone. Therefore Christ alone is our key to Christian living.

Allow me to convey again what I stressed in the opening chapter: If you've trusted Christ, God has *already* placed all of these provisions within you. Each one is a supernatural resource permanently residing within your soul, ready for release every day of your life on earth.

BE PARDONED OR HANG?

In 1829 a man named George Wilson was arrested for robbery and murder in a heist of the U.S. mail. He was tried, convicted, and sentenced to death by hanging. Some friends intervened on his behalf and were finally able to obtain his pardon from President Andrew Jackson. But when Wilson was informed of his pardon, he refused it, saying he wanted to die.

This left the sheriff with quite a dilemma. How could he execute a man who was officially pardoned?

An appeal was made to President Jackson as to what to do. The perplexed president turned the matter over to the U.S. Supreme Court. Chief Justice John Marshall gave this ruling: A pardon is a piece of paper, the value of which depends on its acceptance by the person implicated. Anyone under the sentence of death would hardly be expected to refuse a pardon, but if it is refused, it's no pardon.

Thus George Wilson was executed on the gallows while his signed pardon lay a few hundred feet away on the sheriff's desk!

In the same way, God has offered His gift of divine purity to every person, a gift that not only provides pardon from eternal condemnation but offers much, much more as well. However, this unspeakably marvelous gift must be personally appropriated to be personally beneficial.

"You shall be clean," God promises in the New Covenant. His divine cleansing—this new purity for which only God can receive credit—is the starting point for living out our Christianity. It's what the New Testament calls being "justified," and without it, sanctification (living the Christian life) cannot occur.

So just what does this new purity mean for us? Why is it so important?

THE EXPRESSION ON GOD'S FACE

Fix in your mind the image of God looking down at you day by day. Then honestly answer this question: How would you describe

His facial expression toward you? Is He joyful? sad? disappointed? upset? Is He smiling, frowning, yawning, or just expressionless? Don't worry about being theologically correct; just be honest.

Asking that of myself, I find often that my heart hasn't caught up with what my mind knows to be doctrinally true. When I think of all the failures and missed opportunities in my life, it's hard to imagine God looking down with anything but disappointment written all over His face. That's why the truths in this chapter are so important to me. Time and again I've retreated to them to regain my footing on how God truly sees me.

I believe that many, many Christians feel they're living under God's frown. They can easily relate to the following candid account from a struggling missionary. Can you?

> God's demands of me were so high, and His opinion of me was so low, there was no way for me to live except under His frown.... All day long He nagged me: "Why don't you pray more? Why don't you witness more? When will you ever learn self-discipline? How can you allow yourself to indulge in such wicked thoughts? Do this. Don't do that. Yield, confess, work harder." God was always using His love against me. He'd show me His nail-pierced hands, and then He would look at me glaringly and say, "Well, why aren't you a better Christian? Get busy and live the way you ought to."
>
> Most of all, I had a God who down underneath considered me to be less than dirt. Oh, He made a great ado about loving me, but I believed that the day-to-day love and acceptance I longed for could only be mine if I let Him crush everything that was really me. When I came down to

it, there was scarcely a word or a feeling or a thought or a decision of mine that God really liked.

These words were written before this person had a life-changing encounter with God's grace and a new appreciation of her new purity in Him. But I appreciate her brutal honesty in articulating what many of us have felt in varying degrees.

What does Scripture say about God's expression as He views us? At the risk of sounding irreverent, let me put it this way: *He's smiling from ear to ear!* His fundamental disposition toward you and toward me is that of passionate, loving pursuit and exuberant, unbridled joy. This doesn't mean He isn't displeased over our sinful actions or attitudes. But toward our *person* He is incessantly moving forward in gladsome love.

God's Word makes this promise: "He will rejoice over you with gladness, He will quiet you in His love, He will rejoice over you with singing." Let those words sink deep into your soul—God is singing joyously over you!

Why is this true? *Because when God looks at you He sees Jesus first.* "Your life," after all, "is *hidden* with Christ in God." And God cannot look upon His Son without a smile creasing His face and explosive joy rising in His heart. "This is My beloved Son, in whom I am well pleased," He fairly shouted two thousand years ago. This is what happens today when God looks upon you, because of your permanent submergence in His Son.

In the Chinese language, the word for "righteousness" is the combination of two pictures. On top is the figure of a lamb; directly beneath is that of a person. What a perfect image of the righteousness that Christ alone provides! Whenever the Father looks down at you, He first sees the perfect Lamb of God, "hiding" you. Certainly God is aware of any sin in our lives, but that isn't what He's *primarily* aware of in any believer. What He sees first and foremost is the beauty of His Son enveloping us.

Pause now and try to visualize God smiling broadly as He looks down upon you. Now say to yourself seven times, "God is singing over me with joy!" (If you end up shouting it, that's okay.) The Person who matters most, the Father you'll spend eternity with, the God of unrivaled power—His eyes are now dancing around you with sheer delight as He sings over you, smiling from ear to ear. He cannot do otherwise, for you're united with His Son.

CATASTROPHIC GOODNESS

What else does this wonderful new purity mean for us?

The starting point is the forgiveness of our sins. When God promises in the New Covenant to "remember no more" our sins, it's a figure of speech. Obviously an omniscient God cannot actually forget anything, but He can choose to send our sins away and never, ever hold them against us. The justly deserved penalty for our sins is permanently canceled—not because the charges were dropped, but because they've been paid in full by Someone else.

This forgiveness means that we can look forward with absolute assurance to an endless future spent in that place where "there shall be no more death, nor sorrow, nor crying. There shall be no more pain, for the former things have passed away." Christianity is the only religion that guarantees heaven up-front.

The experience of eternity in God's presence will be so overwhelmingly wonderful that J. R. R. Tolkien coined a great word for it—"eucatastrophe"—incorporating the Greek prefix *eu,* meaning "good." Heaven will be catastrophically good, and catastrophically

good *forever*. Every believer is guaranteed this catastrophic goodness—*no matter what happens after he's trusted Christ for salvation.*

But does the Bible really teach such a risky truth?

SAFE IN HIS GRIP

In a statement from Jesus, we're given three time frames regarding
the absolute certainty of our salvation. Once we've trusted Christ,
three things are immediately and unalterably true.

The first time frame is the present: "Most assuredly," Jesus says,
"he who hears My word and believes in Him who sent Me *has everlasting life.*" We have it now. Already it's ours.

The next time frame concerns the future: "Most assuredly,"
Jesus says, "he who hears My word and believes...*shall not* [literally,
"shall in no possible way"] *come into judgment.*" While every
believer will stand before the judgment seat of Christ for reward
within heaven, none will ever stand before God to be judged in
regards to entrance into heaven.

The third time frame regards our past: "Most assuredly," Jesus
says, "he who hears My word and believes...*has passed from death
into life.*"

On another occasion Jesus said this about His followers: "I give
them eternal life, and *they shall never perish;* neither shall anyone
snatch them out of My hand." We're safe in His grip. Then Jesus
added, "My Father, who has given them to Me, is greater than all;
and no one is able to snatch them out of My Father's hand." We're
in the Father's grip as well!

Is it even theoretically possible to be more eternally secure than
to rest in the grip of the Father and the Son at the same time? No
wonder Christ says we "shall never perish"!

Who Can Really Know for Sure?

Some will say that it's presumptive and arrogant to claim to know that we're saved. Such language *would* be arrogant if we ourselves had anything whatsoever to do with securing our salvation. But there's zero room for our boasting, except in what a great God we have. Our salvation is wholly "the *gift* of God, not of works, lest anyone should boast."

"God has *given* us eternal life," John reminds us, "and this life is in His Son." Our possession of eternal life centers on one issue alone—having Christ in our lives. John continues, "He who has the Son has life; he who does not have the Son of God does not have life." The *only* requirement for knowing that we have eternal life is that we have God's Son in our life through simple faith.

Then John adds another clincher: "These things I have written to you who believe in the name of the Son of God, that you may *know* that you have eternal life." Not "that you may hope," not "that you may guess," not "that you may be fairly sure." He says, "that you may *know*."

You're Discovered!

Besides forgiveness and the assurance of eternal life, our new purity also means we're *cleansed* from those sins. While forgiveness takes care of sin's *penalty*, cleansing takes care of sin's *guilt*. Through forgiveness we escape the torments of hell; through cleansing we escape the torments of conscience.

According to a commonly told story, Sir Arthur Conan Doyle, author of the Sherlock Holmes series, once decided to play a practical joke on twelve of his friends. To each he sent an anonymous telegram that simply read, "Flee at once...all is discovered." Within twenty-four hours, all twelve had fled the country!

All of us, in varying degrees, know what it is to live with such guilt nagging at our consciences, depleting our souls of any real joy. Our flesh has several ways of trying to deal with that guilt. Perhaps the most common is to shift the blame in another direction. Or we try to hide the sins that cause our guilt, perhaps by giving them a softer label: "codependency," "midlife crisis," "personality weakness." We may attempt to bury our guilt through immersion in life's busyness. Or we try making up for our sin through penance—self-punishment.

None of these responses, however, can bring the deep joy of a genuinely cleansed conscience. Only Christ's blood will "cleanse your conscience from dead works." There's no other path to peace within—but it's all ours in our new purity.

OUR ALIEN CLOTHING

And there's more. With God's gift of purity, not only is something infinitely negative—sin's penalty and guilt before God—now taken away, but something infinitely positive is added: We're permanently *clothed* in bestowed righteousness. With all God's people we can declare, "He has clothed me with the garments of salvation, He has covered me with the robe of righteousness."

Luther called this an "alien" or "foreign" righteousness. It's a righteousness wholly belonging to God and wholly bestowed by God, utterly alien to our natural, corrupt state but completely native to God's perfect holiness. And now it's *ours!*

As believers we're more than forgiven sinners; we're saints decked out in the finest wardrobe heaven has to offer. At every moment, in every situation, we're wholly enveloped in God-wrought purity that ensures our Father's unconditional and complete acceptance.

This new purity brings a humble, grateful dignity to the child of God. The dignity comes from the fact that we're now worthy to come boldly before God's throne at all times; the humility comes from the fact that *we* had absolutely nothing to do with this worthiness.

ASSURANCE EVERY MOMENT

So we have it: Our *forgiveness* lets us know we can be *vigorously* assured (we'll talk more about that) of our eternal destiny. We need never fear that some sin might move us out of range from God's grace. As Paul assures us, "Where sin abounded, grace abounded much more." Forgiveness provides the security of our perfect eternal destiny. At any moment when I may doubt I'm really saved, this truth reminds me that assurance is found by focusing upon Christ's cross.

Our *cleansing* lets us know that the Enemy's accusations are forever silenced. At all times we have "hearts sprinkled from an evil conscience and our bodies washed with pure water." At any moment when I feel overwhelmed by guilt, this truth reminds me that I *always* approach God not on the basis of my performance, but solely on the basis of His Son's blood, which has cleansed me from all sin.

The cleansing is total. The story is told that one night the devil approached Martin Luther with a long list of the reformer's sins—lust, greed, and more. Luther, however, pointed out that the list wasn't long enough and proceeded to mention other transgressions the devil should record as well. The list finally completed, Luther told Satan, "Now write at the bottom these words"—and he quoted a statement from the apostle John about God's gift of purity: "The blood of Jesus Christ His Son cleanses us from *all* sin." At that, the devil fled instantly.

And being *clothed* in Christ's righteousness lets us know that we can come boldly before God and His throne of grace. Being robed in the righteousness of Christ provides the humble dignity of God-given significance. At any moment when what seems most real to me is my personal failure, this truth reminds me that my value isn't found primarily in who I am, but in who and what envelopes me.

Wrong God?

The absolute starting point for appreciating our desperate need for this new purity is seeing God aright. This means coming to Him *as He is* and not as we have assumed Him to be or heard Him to be.

Imagine you're talking to someone who admits to knowing nothing about God and who asks you, "What's the first thing I need to know about this God you believe in?" How would you answer?

"He's a loving Father"?

"He's your best Friend"?

"He's an infinitely wise and powerful Being"?

I think it's fair to say that in our day most would go with the image of a loving Father. We expect God to warmly extend His hand from heaven and say something like, "Hello, My name is God. I want you to know I love you and have an abundant life waiting for you." While this is blessedly true, it's no one's first brush with God.

If we follow the pattern of Paul's reasoning in the book of Romans—his most carefully sequenced letter and the New Testament's most comprehensive statement of the gospel—our starting point will be quite different. In the opening chapters of Romans, Paul's overwhelmingly predominant portrait of God is that of a holy and righteous Judge. Astonishingly, *wrath* is the first attribute of God we encounter.

Why does this seem so surprising to many of us?

Several years ago my family attended a social event in our church's gymnasium. As we entered, my youngest son, who was about four, was holding on to my pants leg. By the time we crossed the crowded gym floor, he'd somehow taken hold of another man's pants leg without realizing it. I watched for a moment as my son stood there looking around, clutching confidently. Soon I went closer, got down on one knee, looked him in the eyes, and asked how he was doing. He stared back with great surprise, shot a glance upward to see who he was holding on to, then quickly let go and ran to me. Whoops, wrong dad!

Many people, both believers and unbelievers, are confidently gripping an image of God that simply doesn't square with the God of the Bible. One of the most common of these images is that of a God who is only love and kindness, a kind of deified Mister Rogers. C. S. Lewis said it well:

> We want, in fact, not so much a Father in Heaven as a grandfather in Heaven—a senile old gentleman who, as they say, "liked to see young people enjoying themselves," and whose plan for the universe was simply that it might be truly said at the end of each day, "A good time was had by all."

OFF THE CHART

God is love, but that isn't all God is or all He's capable of. It's a shock for many believers to discover that His most foundational attribute is not love but holiness—the perfect holiness that is the source of His righteous wrath. God's holiness is His "wholly other-ness," His "off the chart-ness." In measuring perfection on a scale of one to ten, God's score is always too astronomical to record. All His other attributes are shot through with this one.

Because of that holiness, one thing is sure: Nobody, but nobody, hugs God when they first encounter Him. We see it throughout Scripture: They quake in His presence; they fall at His feet, face in the dust. The experience shatters them.

"Do you not know," Martin Luther wrote,

> that God dwells in light inaccessible? We weak and ignorant
> creatures want to probe and understand the incomprehen-
> sible majesty of the unfathomable light of the wonder of
> God. We approach; we prepare ourselves to approach. What
> wonder then that his majesty overpowers us and shatters!

Overpowering, shattering—that's exactly who God is. And He remains exactly that, whether or not He's given the go-ahead by you or me.

John White calls him "The God of White-Hot Rage" and wonders if the term sounds extreme.

> Perhaps. But you see, I'm not interested in the kind of God
> we want to believe in, but the God who really is.
>   We Christians are idolaters.... We may not carve him

[God] out of wood, but we do try to forget the uncomfortable parts of him and shape him to our own personal comfort.

I once read an article by a man who called himself an evangelical yet talked about "the kind of God I would feel comfortable with." He at least was being honest about doing what we all do—making God into a sort of holy Teddy Bear....

We are not called to be God's public-relations experts but to be witnesses. The only image we must project is the correct one. We aren't to aim for effect. God's character is not a subject for a media campaign designed to present His best face.

Today our natural propensity isn't so much to carve an idol from wood, but to delete from the true God those attributes we find most uncomfortable or unsettling. We're like children going unattended through a buffet line, piling on our plates only what looks most enjoyable.

"Left to ourselves," A. W. Tozer writes, "we tend immediately to reduce God to manageable terms. We want to get Him where we can use Him, or at least know where He is when we need Him. We want a God we can in some measure control."

The love that provides us with our new purity will never astonish us unless it's seen against the backdrop of God's raging fury toward sin. When He's viewed almost exclusively as a God of love, we see forgiveness as just part of His job. That leaves His love with no punch for us, no fizz, no sparkle. *Assumed grace can never be transforming grace.* We must be primed by the blazing holiness of God before His love and forgiveness will be genuinely life changing.

Are we willing to risk coming to God as He is and not as we would like Him to be? This is no easy step, but if we do, our lives will never be the same.

LION ATTACK

Imagine for a moment we're at a zoo. As we look together at the animals, you reach down over a fence and pet the head of a small lamb. The lamb lifts its head and licks your hand. "That's nice," you think, before we stroll on to see more.

Suddenly you hear me screaming, "Look out!" You turn. Approaching you is the largest, fiercest lion you've ever seen. He's just escaped his cage, and you're his lunch if he so chooses.

There's no escape. He's rushing toward you, his jaws opening ever wider—he's upon you! And he licks your hand, then stands peacefully at your side. You breathe an incredibly deep sigh.

Which lick would mean more to you—that of the lion or that of the lamb? Obviously, the lion's. Why? Because he could just as easily crush you in his jaws, an option the lamb doesn't have.

The primary reason people aren't astonished and exuberant over the Lamb's forgiveness is that they have little or no sense of the Lion's raging fury against their sins. Until we've trembled on death row, we won't dance at the granting of our pardon.

In John's vision in Revelation it is only after he beholds "the Lion of the tribe of Judah" that he sees "a Lamb as though it had been slain." The order is inviolable. Our Lord will never be appreciated as the Lamb unless He's first encountered as the Lion.

HELL

It's because of the Lion's perfect wrath that there's such a place as hell where sinners spend an eternity in torment, although no doctrine is more abhorrent to modern man.

Jonathan Edwards is probably best known for his sermon titled

"Sinners in the Hands of an Angry God." Why did he preach this message on God's everlasting wrath? I agree wholeheartedly with R. C. Sproul's analysis:

> He did this not out of a sadistic delight in frightening people, but out of compassion. He loved his congregation enough to warn them of the dreadful consequences of facing the wrath of God. He was not concerned with laying a guilt trip on his people but with awakening them to the peril they faced if they remained unconverted.

This peril faced by all unbelievers is an *awful* one. The primary image of hell in Scripture is that of "everlasting fire," a fire that "is not quenched." Whether the fire is literal or figurative is really not important. Whatever the punishment is, it's to the soul of man what fire is to his flesh, only more so. No words can possibly describe what it is to face the unrestrained fury of the perfect wrath of the infinite, almighty God.

This state is also *unalterable*. There's no second chance once an unbeliever has passed into eternity. Jesus told how Abraham (with the beggar Lazarus beside him in paradise) answered the miserable cries from Hades of the man who once was rich: "Between us and you," Abraham called, "there is a great gulf fixed, so that those who want to pass from here to you cannot, nor can those from there pass to us." It has been well noted that the rich man at that point became an ardent supporter of missions; he begged Abraham to send Lazarus to testify to the man's five brothers "lest they also come to this place of torment." Hell was so awful he wanted no one he loved to join him there.

This experience of God's wrath will also be *eternal*. It is "everlasting destruction." Unbelievers have no hope of simply being annihilated, consumed out of existence; instead, Jesus described hell as the place where "their worm does not die."

Edwards gave sinners this warning:

> It would be dreadful to suffer this fierceness and wrath of Almighty God one moment; but you must suffer it for all eternity. There will be no end to this exquisite horrible misery. When you look forward, you shall see a long forever, a boundless duration before you, which will swallow up your thoughts, and amaze your soul; and you will absolutely despair of ever having any deliverance, any end, any mitigation, any rest at all. You will know certainly that you must wear out long ages, millions of millions of ages, in wrestling and conflicting with this almighty merciless vengeance: and then when you have so done, when so many ages have actually been spent by you in this manner...you will know that all is but a point to what remains.... Your punishment will indeed be infinite.

All this is why we commit an unspeakably grave offense toward unbelievers when we highlight for them only the love of God and fail to warn them with tears of the horrors lying ahead if they remain unconverted.

STRUCK BY LIGHTNING

Recently my son and I were driving in a thunderstorm when our car was struck by lightning. Immediately the car's horn blared uncontrollably, the lights on the dashboard blinked crazily, the car no longer accelerated, and we smelled smoke from all the wires that had just been fried. And yet, although we saw the flash and heard the rifling crack of thunder, we never *felt* a thing. Inside that car, we were safe.

The wrath of God is far more real and powerful and destructive than that lightning. But on the cross, Jesus took in His own body the full fury of the bolt of that wrath, wrath that *we* had earned. We who are "in Christ" are utterly safe from any possibility of God's wrath striking us. In Christ we'll never feel a trace of the agony He had to bear to perfectly preserve us from the fiery assault of God's wrath. "Jesus paid it all, all to Him I owe."

What a wonder, then, is the gift of God's purity!

I urge you to consider well any aspect of this purity that you may have failed to realize fully before. How do you actually envision the expression on God's face as He watches you on a typical day? From what you've seen in this chapter, is this image a correct one? Are you certain of your eternal salvation? Are you absolutely convinced of your forgiveness, your cleansing, and your being clothed in the righteousness of Christ? Are those truths residing at heart level or only at an intellectual level? And do you comprehend God's righteous wrath enough to be utterly amazed at His gift to you of your new purity? You can rejoice further in these truths as you meditate on the writings of the apostle John in John 10, 1 John 5, and Revelation 5.

CHAPTER 6

Dangerous—and Worth the Risk

*Then suddenly there dawns upon us the vast, entire
endowment of God's free love and forgiveness.... It is
this which bowls us over...frees us...transforms us.*

PAUL TOURNIER

Our New Covenant gift of purity springs from something dangerous, something worth a fresh look—God's grace.

Years ago my family first visited the Grand Canyon. It was a
beautiful, clear day, and the sheer majesty of the sight before me
took my breath away. So did the shortage of guardrails. Our young
boys naturally wanted to race to the very edge and look over. My
instinct was to hold them back, safe from any danger of falling. I
was only too glad to describe the beauty to them if they would stay
back ten yards or so. Somehow they didn't like that idea. After all,
to get the total impact, to fully appreciate the canyon's awesome
beauty, you must go right to the edge.

Grace is like that. If it's to take our breath away and significantly possess our lives, we must go right to the edge—where the
overwhelming astonishment of grace and the potential abuse of
grace linger side by side.

All too often the church has erected safeguards and restrictions to keep people back from the danger of abusing grace and falling into license and lawlessness. In doing so we create an even greater danger—keeping people's view of grace so distant that they fail to have a breathtaking appreciation for the real thing.

IRRATIONAL, UNIMAGINABLE, POWERFUL

If grace makes sense to you, I doubt you're close enough to really see it. The real thing defies comprehension…but not experience. Grace is God's irrational, unimaginable kindness. Yet the word is used so often among believers that we've become callous to its intended impact.

In the New Covenant, God's grace goes beyond anything offered by the world's religions. Virtually all faiths have justice as a primary tenet: Man gets what he deserves (as is particularly true in Islam and Hinduism). Many religions also add the concept of mercy, which is man *not* getting all the punishment he deserves. Christianity alone introduces the full concept of grace—of getting, with no good reason, what we positively *don't* deserve. Grace goes miles beyond mercy.

Grace is the most unreasonable thing in the world. It's also the most powerful. Nothing is more effective for transforming lives, risky though it is.

I well remember my first encounter with grace. I was five years old and our family was on vacation in California. One day at lunch I flatly refused to eat my soup, so my mother said I could have nothing else to eat before dinner.

Late in the afternoon my father and I were running errands together. We stopped in a drugstore where he ordered an ice cream cone, then turned and asked if I'd like one as well. I reminded him of Mom's injunction at lunchtime. With a smile I can still remember, he said he knew what she'd said, but I could still have an ice cream cone if I wanted. Gladly I placed my order.

I don't endorse what my father did as particularly good parenting, but it was my first marvelous experience of clearly getting something I didn't deserve.

One year later my father died of cancer. Today, I can't recall even one spanking he gave me (my mother has assured me there were many), but that event in a California drugstore stays in my memory as my most vivid recollection of him. Burned most deeply into a young boy's psyche was not his father's justice but the precious commodity of grace.

Nothing captures and transforms a person's soul like the power of true grace.

One Saturday morning years ago, I decided to surprise my wife with breakfast in bed. I hurried to a nearby McDonald's and ordered at the drive-through. When I pulled forward to the pickup window, I discovered I was about ninety cents short.

Quite embarrassed, I told the lady at the window I had miscalculated and couldn't buy the meal after all. She asked how much I had. When I told her, she smiled and said that would be enough and handed me my order. I told her I'd go home, get the ninety cents, and come right back to pay her, but she told me not to worry about it. I then promised that the next time I came to that McDonald's I would pay the difference. She laughed and told me to just go home, enjoy breakfast, and quit worrying about what I owed. I drove away, grateful for this token of grace.

The next time I drove down that street looking to grab a fast breakfast, guess where I found myself naturally wanting to go? It was McDonald's—not because I had to or wanted to make up for what I'd done, but simply because I'd received something freely that I in no way deserved and my heart was unable to remain unaffected by it.

Such is the power of genuine grace in any form.

UNRESTRAINED EXUBERANCE

One of the greatest portraits of grace is the father's response to his prodigal son in the story Jesus told. We read that while the son "was still a great way off, his father saw him." We sense that amid his daily work the father had been continually scanning the horizon. Likewise, God's grace isn't something *we* must search for, but something *He* is on the lookout to offer.

Perhaps, as you read these words, God is convicting you of having strayed from Him. Know for sure that He hasn't given up on you; He is, in fact, craning His neck for your return.

We also see in this story the unrestrained exuberance of grace. "His father saw him and had compassion, and ran and fell on his neck and kissed him." In that culture, an older man running toward someone was considered highly undignified. But God's grace is so much more than dignified patience or enduring niceness.

Have you ever pictured God running after you to hold you close and tell you how much He loves you? His grace cannot be tamed or kept in check when one of His beloved comes back to Him. Always He *feels deeply* for us. It's an unbridled passion, the kind that can ignite our own passion toward Him in response.

Consider well this father's embrace of his returning son. It wasn't an extended handshake of guarded love. No, he "ran and fell on his neck and kissed him." The Greek verb tense denotes repeated action—kissing again and again. Yet imagine how this son must have smelled—of swine, of sweat, of days on the dusty road. Repulsive? No more so than when God embraced you and me in all our sin at the cross. There we experienced His divine bear hug, lifting us off our feet, holding us close in spite of our filth.

As the prodigal approached his home, what might he reasonably have expected his father's response to be? Perhaps first of all, a curt command to get cleaned up. Then a stiff lecture laying out the rules for his staying, probationary guidelines, a repayment plan for the squandered wealth. After all, shouldn't forgiveness be extended only when safeguards against its abuse are put in place?

Instead the son found absolutely unconditional forgiveness and acceptance, which is exactly what greets us in our every encounter with our Father.

AN UNCEASING FLOW

In Jesus' story, the grace continues in an unceasing flow. The father tells the servants, "Bring out the best robe...a ring...sandals.... And bring the fatted calf...and let us eat and be merry." Grace is unimaginable in generosity. It gives beyond all reasonable expectation.

The "best" (literally, "first") robe signified special honor. Likewise when you and I came to the foot of the cross for salvation, God not only forgave us but also clothed us with the finest robe available, the righteousness of Christ.

Rings in that day were used to press a seal into wax to validate a transaction. The father's gift of a ring signifies the granting of his authority. It was like giving the son the family credit card. (If this were *your* son, how quickly would you have handed over your American Express?) Grace is willing to take risks that human reasoning never considers.

When you and I trusted Christ, we were given immediate authority to conduct business in the Father's name. Do we deserve this outlandish privilege? Of course not. But then again, nothing in the sphere of grace comes because it's deserved.

The father also called for sandals for the feet of his son, who most likely had returned barefoot. This gift speaks of restored intimacy, for in that day only slaves or the extremely poor went without sandals. The son had come home intending to become his father's slave; before he could even say so, his father reaffirmed his sonship. Despite the rebellion, his relationship with his father had never been in question. He was a son when he left home; he was a son while feeding pigs; he was a son when he returned home; he would be a son forever. Grace alone provides the security of divine relationship that can never be lost.

The Prodigal Father

On top of all this, the father called for a celebration, proving even further his unsparing generosity. In fact, do you know the original definition for the word *prodigal?* We usually think it means "wayward," but it comes from a root that means "excessive or overflowing." A *prodigy* is someone profusely talented; a prodigious writer is known for his vast outflow of words. The son in Jesus' story is called "prodigal" for spending extravagant wealth on extravagant pleasures. But I think this story is really the parable of *the prodigal father*—one who gives to the undeserving with outrageous generosity and irrational kindness. Such is the grace and love of God, surpassing our wildest hopes.

We see this outrageous generosity and irrational kindness of God most clearly in the cross. Here's my own very free translation of Romans 5:8—"God demonstrates His own special brand of love toward us, in that while we were in the pigpen, Christ spilled His precious blood for unworthies such as us."

Such excessive grace doesn't mean God won't sometimes discipline us. But His fundamental, unwavering disposition toward us, His blood-bought children, is relentless, unwavering, wholesale, lavish acceptance. We're now and forever "accepted in the Beloved."

THE POTENTIAL FOR ABUSE

Well now, if that's the way of His grace—if my every sin is more than forgiven—why not give grace a good workout? More fun for me, more glory for God (since I allow Him to demonstrate ever more grace). What a deal! Live like I want to now...then enjoy heaven as well when I die.

That is the *flesh's* response to God's grace. It's a reaction Paul anticipated, and had in fact encountered. "What shall we say then?" he asks rhetorically. "Shall we continue in sin that grace may abound?" Immediately he responds, "Certainly not!" But what are his reasons for that conclusion?

First, notice the reasons he *doesn't* give. Paul nowhere says that if you continue living in sin, you'll lose your salvation. Nor does he say that if you continue in sin, you weren't really saved in the first place.

What he *does* say in essence is this: We should no longer live how we used to live *because we're no longer who we used to be.* He exclaims, "How shall *we who died to sin* live any longer in it?"

Paul, the apostle of grace, was never accused of being a legalist, but he was accused of promoting license. What was true in his day is still true: The faithful proclamation of grace always leads to the charge of antinomianism ("against law"—living any way you please). D. Martyn Lloyd-Jones, the great British pastor and Bible teacher, said that this was in fact "a very good test of gospel preaching"—that it leads to being accused of promoting irresponsible living. "If my preaching and presentation of the gospel of salvation does not expose it to that misunderstanding, then it is not the gospel."

It's true, of course, that grace is sometimes abused, and such abuse is terrible and tragic. Jude speaks of the condemnation of those "who turn the grace of our God into lewdness." But the cure is never to control grace through restrictions and qualifications. *If grace doesn't have the potential to be abused, it won't have the power to transform.* For grace to move powerfully in our lives it must remain unbridled and unrestricted from our well-intentioned safeguards.

For the believer, already cleansed by the blood of Christ, our sin doesn't negate our relationship with God, but it does affect our intimacy with Him. To restore this intimacy requires genuine confession of specific sins. Our new purity through Christ's blood ensures God's everlasting acceptance, while confession of known sins ensures His present communion with our souls.

VIGOROUS ASSURANCE

Earlier I used the term "vigorous assurance" in regard to knowing our eternal destiny. I choose that word *vigorous* as opposed to "tentative" or "partial" assurance. Historically the church has seemed reticent to give believers the kind of full-fledged, out-and-out assurance of salvation that the New Covenant provides. More than for any other reason, this has been done by well-intentioned saints to safeguard the abuse of grace. Their desire to see purity in the church is commendable, but their safeguarding of grace also saps it of its full vitality.

One of the ways we erect these safeguards is to teach that a believer will lose his salvation if he wanders far enough from the Lord. But if we remove the concept of eternal security, we drive a stake right through the heart of grace and drain it of its lifeblood. The absolute assurance of being heaven-bound—solely through God's grace and Christ's righteousness—is the kind of unreasonable kindness that can seize and hold your heart and life like nothing else known to man.

The love and grace that incite such kindness are astonishing beyond words. "Behold what manner of love the Father has bestowed on us," the Bible says. Just exactly what "manner" of love is this? Jesus tells us it's precisely the *same* love with which the Father loves Jesus, His only begotten Son. "You have sent Me," He prayed, "and have loved them *as* You have loved Me."

Such a concept—that God's love for me matches His love for Christ—seems impossible if not heretical. Yet this is what Scripture says.

How can it be true? One reason is that *perfect, eternal love is incapable of loving at varying degrees.* God loves at only one level—perfection. Another reason is that God loves us *because of who He is, not who we are.* His love for us is unchanging because God is unchanging—always faithful in His commitment toward us.

PUTTING OUR NEW PURITY TO WORK

How do we take hold of this grace experientially? In a word, it's by *faith.*

Luther called faith "the 'yes' of the heart." How do you think of it?

I believe the essence of faith is dependence, a dependence rooted in a genuine and overwhelming sense of need. That's why the Sermon on the Mount begins, "Blessed are the poor in spirit, for theirs is the kingdom of heaven." Brokenness and faith are so closely intertwined, it's difficult to tell where one ends and the other begins.

Several years ago our church's college group was studying Romans. Among these students was a young woman who grew up in a strong Christian home, had gone to a Christian school, and was now involved in several Christian activities on campus. She was engaged to a seminary student and was on her way to becoming a pastor's wife. About halfway into the semester she announced to her small group that she'd just become a Christian. At first they laughed, but she told them she was dead serious. While studying Romans she had realized for the first time that *she* was a sinner. She had known that Christ died for sinners, but she had never truly counted herself among that group until the Spirit of God opened her eyes to her own sinfulness. Only then did she genuinely believe.

TURNING AWAY, TURNING TOWARD

True faith also requires that we consciously empty our hands of all personal merit if we're to genuinely take hold of the cross and experience God's gift of our new purity. We don't have saving faith if we come to Christ believing that salvation is a combination of trusting Him *plus* something else—baptism, living a moral life, church attendance, whatever. We must *turn away* from any wrong object of trust. This is the fundamental idea behind the word *repentance,* which literally means "to change the mind."

In true faith we also *turn to* the right object of trust—and only Christ is worthy of our trust. Only by embracing the Person of Christ can our new purity be received and known. "For Christ is the end of the law for righteousness to everyone who believes."

Imagine you're desperately thirsty and a cup of clear, cold water is placed before you. You're definitely aware of what's there; you're also certain that it can quench your thirst. But when does it actually make a practical difference in your life? Only when you receive it—in other words, *drink.* Until then your thirst remains untouched, no matter how firmly you give mental assent to the reality and significance of that cold water in front of you. To genuinely believe is not only to agree, but also to appropriate.

SAVING FAITH?

We must be careful to call people to exercise this true faith as we present the gospel. "Faith," wrote J. Gresham Machen, "consists not in doing something, but in receiving something."

Suppose you're with a friend, and the conversation takes a spiritual turn. You probe a little, and your friend says he "gave his life" to Christ at a church camp when he was fifteen, but he has never felt really sure that it "took." Where would you go from there?

A good place to start would be the standard diagnostic question, "Let's suppose you and I died tonight and we both went before God. If God were to ask you, 'Why should I let you into heaven?' how would you answer Him?"

When I ask that question and the person's response includes anything whatsoever about being a good person or doing good things, I immediately assume he isn't saved. I may find out later that he is a Christian and was just fuzzy in his beliefs, but most often that isn't the case.

Gospel invitations that present becoming a Christian as a matter of "giving" or "surrendering" your life to Christ often confuse the real issue. Although God clearly calls every believer to all-out surrender to Christ as Lord, this comes only *after* the person has been made a new creation in Christ and has the resources necessary for such a life. To require the unbeliever to give his all to Christ is like telling a man with no legs to get up and walk. Someone who's spiritually dead cannot enlist in a spiritual army. He must first receive new life.

Notice the object of faith we're emphasizing when we tell others they must give their life to Christ in order to be saved. Their faith is being directed toward *what I must do for Christ* rather than what Christ has done for me.

Over the years I've talked to several people who "gave their lives to Christ" but never became Christians. How is that possible? In each case their faith was resting on what they had done for God (self-surrender), not on what He had done for them in giving His Son.

We haven't given people the true gospel until we point out a Person to receive and fully trust, rather than a lifestyle to follow. Once they receive that Person, He immediately infuses them with the desire and power for the new lifestyle He requires.

How We View Others

This new purity has momentous impact on how I view others. It tells me, for example, that there are no insignificant believers.

Each one's worth is forever secured by the blood of Christ shed for them.

Once Paul was captured by Christ, he forever saw believers in light of their divine purity, not their sinful flesh. Acknowledging that some of the Corinthian believers had been "fornicators," "idolaters," "adulterers," "homosexuals," "thieves," "covetous," "drunkards," "revilers," and "extortioners," he immediately affirms, "But *you were washed*, but *you were sanctified*, but *you were justified* in the name of the Lord Jesus and by the Spirit of our God." Our new purity enables me to view myself and all other believers through the new lenses of imputed righteousness.

It also reminds me that no unbeliever should be dismissed as worthless. "God has shown me," Peter said, "that I should not call any man common or unclean." The most obnoxious, hateful, irritating heathen is still someone Christ came to die for. God calls me to pray for them, serve them, and strive for their acceptance of Christ's death.

SECURE ENOUGH TO LOVE

We begin taking the risks that genuine love requires—and launching out into the joyous adventure of such love—only when our own hearts are resting securely in a surplus of love that can never be removed. Our God-bestowed security is the foundation for loving others well.

Only secure people can love well. Only through the God-bestowed security of our new purity can our souls be freed from enslavement to others' acceptance and approval.

It's only natural that I *desire* your acceptance; there's nothing wrong or sinful in that. But when I cease deriving my full acceptance from Christ, I'll begin to *require* and *strive* for your acceptance. To the degree I do that, I'm incapacitated from loving you well.

This insecurity may exhibit itself in a pushy, grasping style of relating that openly criticizes your not being more caring toward me. Or it may come through in a quiet fear, refusing to ruffle feathers lest your acceptance of me be jeopardized. In either case, my ability to love you fully is sabotaged.

All this is why it's so important to feast constantly on God's love as seen at the cross. As we profoundly sense our own forgiveness and acceptance, we'll be released to freely extend the same toward others.

Before we move on to the second great provision of the New Covenant, I encourage you to evaluate how God's gift of your new purity is affecting your life, especially your view toward others and your relationships with them. Are you living enough in the rich and grateful experience of God's grace to impart this same grace to others? *Only grace-soaked saints can become grace-dispensing servants.*

As you think about that, I encourage you to read and meditate on Luke 15 or Romans 4 and 5.

CHAPTER 7

Releasing Your New Identity

The moment I consider Christ and myself as two, I am gone.

MARTIN LUTHER

Grace is risky business. It's the most soul-intoxicating, life-transforming commodity in the universe. Nothing rivals its ability to turn sinners into saints. Unfortunately, as we've seen, it can also be abused by saints who continue trafficking in sin. Surely God has erected some safeguards or barriers to keep us from taking advantage of His good nature.

But we saw that when Paul addressed this thorny issue of why we should not "continue in sin that grace may abound," he did not erect a safeguard. Instead he laid a foundation to launch us into holiness. That foundation is the radical, actual new personhood gifted us at our conversion. It's time to explore in depth that new personhood.

On one hand, we'll discover that *we're no longer who we used to be.* Equally we'll find that *we're now what we never were.* Grace has permanently changed not only our eternal destiny but also our present identity.

I opened this book with the story of the golden eagle who spent his days living like a prairie chicken, unaware that his lifestyle was out of sync with who he really was. As long we view ourselves fundamentally as sinners (though forgiven), then soaring, saintly living will appear over our heads and out of reach; we'll stay trapped in prairie-chicken living.

THREE FUNDAMENTAL CHANGES

Let's quickly get the big picture here.

At conversion three things were radically altered simultaneously. First is what happened *legally.* We went from being guilty before an infinitely holy God to being fully forgiven and acquitted of all crimes.

Second, there was a radical change *relationally.* We went from being condemned slaves to adopted children—"you received the Spirit of adoption by whom we cry out, 'Abba, Father.'"

Third, there was a radical change *inherently.* Something happened to our deepest internal nature. We went from being "by nature children of wrath" to being "partakers of the *divine nature.*" The intrinsically wicked part of us is now offset (not removed) by an intrinsically perfect nature belonging to God Himself. Our *condition* has changed as well as our *position.* We're now thoroughly renovated saints.

WHAT NO PILL CAN DO

Imagine a courtroom where a newly convicted criminal is standing, about to be sentenced for his crimes. Suddenly the judge looks away from the criminal and calls his son to the bench. The gavel comes crashing down, and the judge pronounces the criminal "not guilty" because his son has agreed to serve the sentence in full. This represents, of course, the first aspect of our conversion, justification. Our legal debt before God has been paid in full.

Then the judge steps down from the bench, puts His arm around the criminal, and tells him he wants to adopt him into his family. "You're coming home with us," the judge says warmly. This is the next aspect of our conversion, our adoption.

But the third aspect of our conversion—our inner renovation—is something no human judge could ever possibly do. The criminal may walk out of that courtroom forgiven and adopted, but he's still fundamentally the same person as before. There's no pill the judge can give him to cause the criminal to actually *want* to do right from now on, something to offset the man's criminal inclinations.

Yet this is exactly what God has done in our rebirth. We're changed *inherently* as well as legally and relationally, through what Paul calls "the washing of *regeneration* and *renewing* of the Holy Spirit."

Costume Jewelry or Tarnished Silver?

Costume jewelry is essentially worthless metal covered with an attractive coating. So many believers see themselves in that way—sinners through and through, yet covered by the blood of Christ.

Tarnished silver is a much truer image of who we are after conversion. While we're covered by the infinite righteousness of Christ, we're also new creations in Christ (silver) clothed in an earth suit that is sin-saturated (tarnished). The new you isn't a sinner but rather a saint who struggles with the tarnish of sin.

One night my wife and I were having a fairly heated discussion over a particular habit of mine that annoyed her. As the discussion continued, I became angrier and more defensive, a reaction Sandy didn't understand.

Finally I realized I was attaching her criticisms to my essential identity, which was causing me to feel threatened. However, it wasn't *me* she was finding fault with, but only a particular behavior of mine.

God brought a picture to my mind. "So," I told Sandy, "it's not like you're saying I'm ugly, but just pointing out that my hair's out of place."

"That's *exactly* what I'm saying," she responded. She went on to again affirm my true identity (something she's so good at), which made it much easier for me to hear her comments about my annoying habit.

This picture has helped me many times since then. As Christians we all have our hair out of place in different ways, but *no believer is fundamentally ugly.* That's true because, at our conversion, we received far more than forgiveness and a new eternal destiny; we also received an internal, unalterable *transformation.* A supernatural revolution within has occurred. You're not merely a forgiven sinner; you're a "new creation."

What's truly *primary* to us as believers is our divinely implanted righteousness; sin is now only secondary. "Saintness" is not only your position (through justification and adoption), it's also your condition. "Saintness" is your state as well as your status. Sin is still resident in our overall condition, but it's no longer the primary homeowner.

Therefore, "The Christian life is simply the process of becoming who we are," as someone ably expressed it. We don't change our living in order to become godly; we change our living because we've already been made godly. We stop scratching around like prairie chickens, not in order to *become* golden eagles, but because we really *are* golden eagles.

SWALLOWED UP

This new identity is entirely ours because of our union with Christ. After Paul declares to the Corinthians, "You are *in* Christ Jesus," he immediately summarizes what Christ Himself "became for us"; Jesus Himself became our "wisdom from God" and our "righteousness and sanctification and redemption." This is a passage to feast on.

Our new identity is *a Christ-saturated identity.* Hear the words again: *You are in Christ Jesus.* As believers we no longer have the option of thinking of ourselves as separate from Him. We're wholly swallowed up in Him.

"Your life," Paul says, "is hidden with Christ in God." Jesus Christ "*is* our life," he adds. Our assimilation is so radical that it's virtually impossible to tell where we begin or He ends. He *is* our life and therefore the strength of our identity, its center and circumference.

JESUS OUR WISDOM

Our new identity is also *a Christ-sufficient identity.* All we'll ever need to live life as God designed it—*everything* for time and eternity—is supplied through our inseparable union with Christ.

Do you see yourself as unskilled and unproductive in grasping the things of God? Then remember Paul's words that Jesus Himself has become *your* "wisdom from God."

Although I'd become a Christian a few years earlier, I first started truly walking with the Lord in my early twenties (tennis had been my whole life up to that point). As I began spending time with other committed believers, I easily became intimidated by the amount of Bible knowledge and spiritual wisdom they evidenced. They knew all kinds of passages by heart; about the only thing I knew was that Jesus loved me. Their Bibles were falling apart from use, and some had even had their Bibles rebound, which to me was almost unbelievable. I wrestled with the deep feelings of spiritual inferiority as I compared myself to them.

One night during that time I was trying to study my Bible but feeling little sense of progress. I lowered my forehead to my desk and prayed something to the effect of, "Lord, you know I'm nothing but a dumb jock. I just can't get what everyone else seems to get. If I'm going to know You or gain any wisdom, You're going to have to *give* it to me, because I clearly can't get it on my own."

Only years later did I discover that understanding the Scriptures spiritually, not just academically, is impossible apart from Christ's presence and the ministry of His Spirit. But from that night on, any spiritual wisdom I've gleaned over the years from Scripture has always felt far more like a gift than an acquisition. Certainly I've tried to study diligently and utilize the original languages. But every significant discovery has come chiefly through desperate reliance on Christ to open my mind and heart.

I no longer see myself as dumb. I don't really think of myself as smart, either. I see myself simply as someone merged with the wisdom of Christ, enjoying what God has given me while recognizing that an endless ocean of His wisdom still lies before me.

GETTING USED TO JUSTIFICATION

Do you see yourself as unworthy and sinful? Then remember Paul's declaration that Jesus Himself has become *your righteousness.* In

God's eyes you're whiter than the freshly fallen snow and purer than the clearest stream.

The righteousness of God not only covers you but also indwells you. "Christ is made unto us inherent as well as imputed righteousness," wrote Jonathan Edwards. Does the Christian life seem to require too much of you? Do His commands seem utterly overwhelming? Then remember God's affirmation that Jesus Himself has become *your sanctification.*

This sanctification is a gift as well as a process. When we're born again we receive a new nature that's already sanctified; the *process* of sanctification is merely the ongoing unveiling of this gifted sanctification. Someone put it like this: "Sanctification is simply the art of getting used to justification."

Do you see yourself as being in such difficult circumstances that you have no hope of being delivered? Then remember God's truth that Jesus Himself has become *your redemption.* He provides, as Edwards said, "actual deliverance from all misery, and the bestowment of all happiness and glory."

A Relaxed Self-Image

This inexhaustible sufficiency of Christ is what allows us to have a joyful and relaxed self-image, one that isn't grasping for proof of personal adequacy. Our sense of self is now God-derived, God-sustained, God-absorbed, God-glorifying. What frees us from the paralyzing grip of inferiority and inadequacy is not the power of positive thinking but the power of this united identity with Christ.

What we experience is not better *self-esteem* but genuine *Christ-esteem.* We humbly enjoy our new identity and thank God for it. Yet we glory not in *it,* but in *the Lord* who gave it. After Paul tells us that Christ Himself has become our wisdom and righteousness and sanctification and redemption, he draws our attention to the higher purpose—"that, as it is written, 'He who glories, let him glory in the LORD.'" All the recognition for our new identity must go to Christ.

This is why we're not to be preoccupied with developing a good self-image. We already have the best one available. "God has given us something far more fascinating to think about than ourselves," as Oswald Chambers once put it. We're to be preoccupied with the beauty and "spectacularness" of Christ and how we can best display it in everyday living.

WITH HIM IN DEATH

When we trust Christ for salvation we become inseparably united with Christ in four dimensions of His existence.

First, we become united with Him *in His death* on the cross two thousand years ago. This is what Paul meant in saying, "I have been crucified with Christ." *You* also died on that cross at Calvary; we're "born crucified" (in L. E. Maxwell's words) when we become Christians.

Do you find this difficult to comprehend? It's not difficult; it's *impossible*. But we don't have to wholly understand it to experience it, just as I drive my car each day without fully understanding most of what makes it work. We simply need to trust that we've shared in Christ's death, because God says so.

Our death on the cross with Christ is what sets *us* free from sin's power and dominion over us. "Our old man was crucified with Him," Paul says, "that the body of sin might be done away with, that we should no longer be slaves of sin." The Greek word translated here as "done away with" could be better expressed as "rendered inoperative" or "put out of business." The point is not that sin is *eradicated* but *incapacitated*.

It's not that sin has ceased to be real and very present, but it has ceased to be the inevitable master. Sin's power over us was "put out of business" when we died with Christ on His cross. Temptations are no problem for dead people.

But while we've died to sin, *nowhere does the Scripture say that sin has died to us.* The fundamental meaning of death is "separation." Because of our death with Christ we've become separated from sin's power, although that power is in no way extinguished. We can still choose to reconnect ourselves to sin's dominion, but the Cross has given us the freedom to choose otherwise. This is why Scripture commands, "Reckon yourselves to be dead indeed to sin." Our responsibility is not so much to mortify the flesh as to remember our death and act upon it. Ruth Paxson put it well: "Sin need have no more power over the believer than he grants it through unbelief. If he is alive unto sin it will be due largely to the fact that he has failed to reckon himself dead unto sin."

Buried with Him

We're also united with Christ in His burial—"buried with Him in baptism," as Paul expresses it. We're merged into Christ's experience in the tomb. God has buried the old you with His Son. This, too, is why we aren't the same person coming out of conversion that we were going in. The person we were before is left inside the tomb with the graveclothes. As Paul says, "Old things have passed away; behold all things have become new."

We're no longer who we used to be. Let those words sink deeply into your soul. God's way of dealing with our past is not recovery, but *burial.* This is why the "fix what is wrong" model is inherently flawed. God has no intention of fixing what He has buried.

If you were an alcoholic going into conversion, you weren't one when you came out. You may still struggle with alcohol, even intensely, but in your essential personhood you are *not* an alcoholic. You're a new creation in Christ whose flesh is especially tempted by drink, but the real you is "created according to God, in true righteousness and holiness."

If you were the victim of a dysfunctional home (who isn't, to one degree or another?) your victim-identity did not remain intact after regeneration. It was shredded at the Cross. You may still struggle in your flesh with the effects of your home life. But your true identity has nothing to do with past dysfunction and everything to do with present Christ-oneness. In Christ you actually have *a new past, a new family* (the body of Christ), and *a new Father.*

Whatever the reality of your own past, it's no longer the deepest reality of your present. Your background is buried with Christ.

Resurrected with Him

The third dimension is our union with Christ's resurrection. "You were raised with Christ," Paul states. We're inseparably united to the same power that raised Christ from the dead.

Through our crucifixion and burial with Christ, we're no longer who we used to be; through union with His resurrection *we now are who we never were.* Every believer is a walking miracle, the scene of resurrection power. This is why Paul says, "Just as Christ was raised from the dead by the glory of the Father, even so we also should walk in newness of life."

Whatever God calls us to in this life is to be carried out in reliance upon the Lord's grave-busting power, a power that's always present.

STILL ALIVE, STILL AT WORK

The fourth dimension is our union with Christ's present life. "It is no longer I who live," Paul writes, "but *Christ lives* in me."

We're united with One who not only has a perfectly stellar past but also a perfectly stellar present. Christ didn't stop living for God after He was resurrected and ascended; He's at work on earth (through His Spirit and His people), and He's at work in heaven, where "He always lives to make intercession for them." Christ right now is living as fully and working as passionately for His Father's glory as ever. This fully engaged Christ now dwells within us, One with whom we're supernaturally incorporated. We live unto God because we're one with Him who never stops living for His Father. We've simply come along for the ride, so to speak.

Our life is not trying to "live for" Christ; our life *is* Christ Himself. This is why the New Covenant was given: Christ for our past, Christ for our present, Christ for our future.

In Christ's death and burial we find God's provision for our *past* identity; in Christ's resurrection and life we find His provision for our *present* identity:

The life that once He lived on earth,
He lives again in me.

The Right Path

This radical, actual new personhood given to us at conversion is our true foundation for godly living. In the book of Romans, after Paul explains our justification (in chapter 5), he takes pains (in chapters 6 and 7) to show us what it means specifically to be a new creation in Christ *before* moving on to talk about the Holy Spirit's role in our sanctified living (chapter 8).

So often in the church today we try to rush people immediately from Romans 5 to Romans 8 and bypass the message of Romans 6 and 7. But after recognizing our new purity (justification), God wants us focus next on our new identity. Then we'll see all of life in a new light. We won't view God's commands merely as a list of "shoulds," but as trails leading to a soul satisfaction and personal significance found nowhere else on earth.

How have you viewed yourself? As a forgiven sinner, but still a sinner through and through? Or as a renovated saint? As you give attention to all that's true about your new identity, how can you fully express this in praise and worship to Jesus, your Lord and Savior, who *is* your life? To help you do this, meditate on the truths of Romans 6 and 1 John 3.

CHAPTER 8

Your Newness Goes Public

God became man to turn creatures into sons; not simply to produce better men of the old kind but to produce a new kind of man.

C. S. LEWIS

Fall in New England—there's nowhere I'd rather be to see the leaves changing colors. As someone who grew up among the more subdued hues of West Texas, I find few things on earth more stunningly beautiful than the brilliant red, orange, and yellow of the northeastern autumn landscape.

A few years ago I discovered something interesting about how those leaves change color. In essence, they don't. All spring and summer each leaf's true color is masked over by green chlorophyll cells. When fall comes and the chlorophyll departs, the true color is no longer obscured. The "change" is really just an unveiling. The leaf doesn't become more colorful; it shows the world what it has been all along.

That, my friend, is the essence of true spirituality. Christian growth—our sanctification—is the continued unveiling of the full array of our true colors, colors that were divinely and unalterably given us the instant we trusted Christ. These colors are nothing less than those of God Himself.

That's why our further maturing in Christ—our sanctification—is simply *becoming who we are,* as we said in the last chapter. Our life's story becomes the continuing saga of our new creation state going public. Let's now explore more deeply the practical ramifications of that unveiling.

YOUR SCAR

A scientific researcher once got ten volunteers to participate in an experiment to study how people respond to a stranger with a physical deformity—in particular, an unsightly facial scar.

The experiment proceeded separately for each volunteer. A makeup artist applied the ugly "scar," then the person was shown his or her image in a handheld mirror before being sent to a medical office waiting room to sit and observe people's reactions.

However, just before each person was sent out, the makeup artist deftly erased the scar altogether under the guise of applying a finishing touch of powder to keep the scar from smearing. None of the volunteers realized this last-second change. And all ten later reported the same kind of reactions in the waiting room: People were rude, shunned them, and kept staring at their scars!

More than we're aware, we view others and their responses to us through how we see ourselves. For believers, that picture is often quite inaccurate in light of God's truth.

IS GOD TELLING THE TRUTH ABOUT YOU?

The key issue for every believer is not whether our sense of identity is good or poor, but whether it's accurate. Do we believe God is telling the truth when He describes the revolution within us at our conversion?

"You are *complete* in Him," Paul says about the practical result of our oneness in Christ. The Greek word here most literally means "having been made *full.*" You've been literally filled with every resource for walking the path of discipleship.

GOD'S VERY NATURE WITHIN

This is why a good self-image is not *developed* but rather *received.* We aren't called to figure out new ways to think positively about ourselves, but to humbly and gratefully trust what God says about who we are in Christ. Our true identity is as much a gift from God as getting into heaven—and just as real. And it's ready *now* to be applied.

I just finished making a difficult phone call. It concerned a fairly messy and complicated situation with the potential of becoming ugly, and I felt wholly inadequate to handle it. I dreaded the call and kept putting it off all day.

What helped me most to finally dial the number was reminding myself of what God has placed within me. My inadequacies aren't all there is to me; within me there resides *God's very nature* of love, compassion, boldness, and wisdom, and this is actually more central to who I am than any of my shortcomings.

This was my sole hope for handling the call in a God-honoring fashion. I trusted God to provide what I needed to glorify Him and to love the person I would be talking with. With genuine reliance on Him, I made the call, although still a bit reluctantly.

How did it go? Okay. Not great. Not terrible. On the whole I felt I was simply releasing what God had put within me. There were times I felt my flesh coming into play and I became tentative, but overall my spoken words and tone seemed like God's doing. I don't know what the results of the call will be, but that's not the issue. I sensed God's flowing, and in that I rest gratefully.

TESTING YOUR SELF-IDENTITY

What keeps us from deeply tapping into our new identity?

One of our biggest hindrances is *labeling.* If I say to myself, "You're just a procrastinator," I'm labeling my fundamental identity. This is very different from saying, "You're procrastinating," which is honestly pointing out behavior without attacking identity.

Our only accurate labels are those we find in the Scriptures that portray our new identity—we're "in Christ," "a new creation," "partakers of the divine nature," "complete" in Christ, "the fragrance of Christ," Christ's "workmanship," "children of God," "heirs of God," "more than conquerors," and so on.

Is that how you most frequently see yourself? Or are you guilty of sticking on wrong labels?

Here's a test: Ask yourself, What role, responsibility, or aspect of my life has the potential to trigger in me the deepest disappointment as well as the highest happiness? If you're a parent, it might be your children's behavior more than anything else that can cause you either to soar with pride or die of embarrassment. If so, your primary identity label is probably that of a mother or father. Your children's conduct then becomes the real barometer of your personal worth and significance, and you may find yourself trying to control your children rather than releasing them in God's direction.

Here's another way to help pinpoint your primary sense of identity: Write (or mentally imagine) your first and last names on a piece of paper, followed by a blank. Now fill in that blank with the word that first comes to mind after saying your name. Be brutally honest. There's a good chance that whatever thought comes first represents the self-identity you hold most deeply.

More Wrong Labels

What are the inadequate labels we most often put in that blank?

One of the most common (especially for men) is our occupation—mechanic, accountant, teacher, programmer. But God never intended our occupation to become our primary source of identity. If we do, we let occupation override *vocation*—our calling to glorify God as comprehensively as possible. If my own primary identity is that of "pastor," I'll be more concerned about the appearance and size of "my" church than about advancing God's kingdom. When someone leaves the church, my sense of personal worth will be at stake.

Asked what she did for a living, a woman answered, "I'm a disciple of Jesus Christ disguised as a secretary." She was finding her identity in the right place.

We can also gravitate to a host of other self-labels. For some, it's a personality type or temperament ("Type A," "high I," "melancholic"). For others, it's a psychological condition, an addiction, a disability, or a past hurt: "manic-depressive," "schizophrenic," "alcoholic," "codependent," "ADHD," "dyslexic," "incest victim," "broken home victim"—the list is practically endless.

Such conditions and situations can be only too real, their pain only too piercing. There's adversity and tragedy in the backgrounds and present circumstances of countless Christians, and these deeply affect them. But the issue is this: *Where* has it affected them?

No Christian has a damaged soul. What we all have is wrinkled flesh—flesh in the sense of our fallen, sinful nature. Pain in our past leaves *no imprints whatsoever* on our new creation state, but it can cause our flesh to react in self-protective or self-gratifying ways.

This doesn't mean there's no place for looking at our past, but our purpose should be to find whatever hinders us from more fully appropriating our supernatural present. (We often need assistance in seeing the lies that block the way; a godly counselor or shepherd can be immeasurably helpful here.)

No Christian need ever stand up in an Alcoholics Anonymous meeting and declare, "I am an alcoholic." It simply isn't true. He may be struggling with alcohol addiction, but he himself is not an alcoholic. The real him is a new creation garbed in alcohol-craving flesh. The starting point for real victory is recognizing that his real identity thirsts for righteousness much more than for alcohol.

The same is true for all other addictions, as well as any mental or physical disabilities. No such limitation is a Christian's true identity. My son, who has cerebral palsy, is not a cerebral palsic (if there is such a word). He's a disciple of Jesus whose temporary physical body doesn't move as well as that of most others. His true identity isn't affected one iota by the disability with which God has entrusted him on this earth.

Your bad habits, your personality profile, your "problems," your "tendencies"—these things are never your core identity. God has seen to it that something far better is at the center of your personhood. "Should anyone knock at my heart," wrote Martin Luther, "and say, 'Who lives here?' I should reply, 'Not Martin Luther, but the Lord Jesus Christ.'" There's no pride whatsoever in seeing yourself this way, for your new identity in Christ is wholly the work of God. And now God calls you to humbly and joyously embrace it.

"IT IS NOT I"

One of the most common labels with which Christians wrongly tag themselves is that of a sin—"adulterer," "drunkard," or whatever. As we genuinely take hold of who we are in Christ, we'll see our sin in a new light.

You'll recall my earlier mention of Greg and his struggle with homosexuality. Greg told me that one day he was reading in 1 Corinthians 6, where Paul lists homosexuality and several other sins of the Corinthians. When his eyes fell on the words, "and such *were* some of you," a light went on in his heart. For the first time he realized that now he *is not* a homosexual but a new creation in Christ whose flesh happens to struggle with homosexuality. This realization, more than anything else, led to Greg's truly remarkable and supernatural turnaround.

Before Augustine of Hippo was converted to Christianity, he was very immoral sexually. The story is told that, not long after he'd become a believer, he was walking down a side street when a woman came up quietly behind him. "Augustine, it is I," she whispered; he recognized her as someone with whom he'd been sexually involved.

Augustine turned to her and replied, "Yes, but it is not I." He knew he was no longer the man he used to be.

So it is for every believer. When we don't recognize this truth, the results are tragic.

WEAPONS FOR THE WAR

The story is told of a man on a psychiatrist's couch who explained, "When I go grocery shopping and walk past the dog food section, I have this overwhelming urge to rip open an Alpo bag and start eating."

Here was something the doctor had never encountered. He asked when his patient first began noticing this urge.

"I'm not really sure," the man replied. "I think ever since I was a puppy."

I know it's a dumb joke, but it makes an important point. If you believe you're a dog, dog food will seem both reasonable and necessary. And if you believe you're still fundamentally a sinner, *sin will seem both reasonable and necessary.* When sin feels inevitable, it's almost always because we aren't in tune with our true identity.

Our union with Christ provides freedom from sin's shackles. Sin has become genuinely unnecessary. It's now an option rather than a certainty. Sin is not lust encountered, but lust obeyed.

Sin is also utterly inappropriate to our new identity. Having been supernaturally renovated to "walk in newness of life," we are now to display our new wardrobe of divine royalty. To continue living in sin would be like the queen of England going around in the tattered and dirty garb of a bag lady.

Furthermore, sin is wholly insane because of our new identity. Paul says of sin, "The end of those things is death." No matter what sin promises up-front, it always brings a deadening to our lives—loss of joy, loss of peace, fear of being found out, and so on.

Sin for the believer is nothing better than chocolate-covered Alpo. It may bring momentary pleasure, but the aftertaste will kill you. To go for Alpo when the choicest steak is available is foolish beyond words. Until we understand that sin is as foolish as it is wrong, we probably won't change. Nothing helps us see that better than grabbing hold of who we really are now that Christ indwells us.

LIKE ANGELS INSIDE

Everything we've learned about labeling ourselves is just as true in how we view other believers.

This is especially so for our children who are saved. I was having a heated discussion one evening with one of my sons about why we needed a filtered Internet provider for our home computer. It makes Internet access extremely slow, but I explained the dangers (particularly the sexual ones) of not having a filter. With three teenage boys, the testosterone level at our house is off the chart anyway; no need to add fuel to the fire.

My son wasn't buying that. Frustrated with my reasoning, he finally said, "Dad, the problem is that you really don't trust me, do you?"

"Son," I answered, "I trust *you*. I really do. But I don't trust your hormones."

His demeanor changed immediately. The anger seemed to evaporate. He felt less threatened and could look at himself more objectively. We continued our conversation productively, admitting that neither of us can trust our own hormones.

One of the greatest gifts we can give other Christians, including our believing children, is to affirm their new identity continually and never confuse it with their flesh. According to a commonly told story, Michelangelo once was struggling to transport a huge piece of stone when a bystander asked why he would go to all that trouble for an "old piece of rock." The artist replied, "Because there is an angel in there that wants to come out." This is how we're to see one another. We all have rough edges, but Christ dwells inside each of us, awaiting full release.

Spiritual Beings in a Human Experience

"We are not human beings having a spiritual experience," someone has noted. "We're spiritual beings having a human experience."

Where exactly have you been finding your primary sense of identity? Have you been tagging your deepest self with inadequate labels that are merely human, rather than the spiritual labels God has provided through your new creation in Christ?

How are you viewing sin? Are you continuing in any sins because you haven't seen them as truly unnecessary in your life, fully inappropriate, and entirely foolish?

As you consider these questions, I encourage you to meditate on Colossians 3 and Ephesians 2.

CHAPTER 9

Releasing Your New Disposition

*When the law is written in the heart...it means that the love of God's law
and of Himself has now become the moving power of our life.... However
cold or feeble we may feel, faith knows that the new heart is in us,
that the love of God's law is our very nature, that the teaching and power
of the Spirit are within us. Such faith knows it can obey.*

ANDREW MURRAY

Liver is one of my least favorite foods. My problem is with the
taste, or perhaps distaste is a better way to put it. I grew up dread-
ing those nights Mom fixed liver for dinner, encouraging us with,
"It's good for you." Those words meant nothing to me, and they
certainly did nothing to make liver more palatable.

I've tried smothering it with ketchup or gulping it down with a
bite of something else on my plate, but the liver flavor always
seemed stronger than everything else. Nothing has ever come close
to helping me like it.

I doubt that liver itself will ever be radically and substantively
changed to taste like steak or hamburger. So for me to actually
enjoy eating it, only one option seems to remain. I suppose it's con-
ceivable that I could undergo a tongue transplant and be given the

tongue of a liver-lover. My new set of taste buds could then rejoice in liver rather than merely endure it. Liver would no longer be an "ought to" but a "get to."

When you and I became believers, something similar happened to us. We were given a heart transplant that instilled a whole new set of God-given desires. God has seen to it that our new, regenerate hearts will incessantly and instinctively yearn for the best things in all the universe—Himself and His glory, His will and His words. This is every saint's innate longing, a hunger that goes unsatisfied at any other table but God's.

It's "a holy, heavenly disposition," as Jonathan Edwards termed it. Because of it, the will of God isn't just an "ought to" anymore, but also a "want to." Because of our revolution within, obeying Him has become not only our moral duty, but also our new heart's truest and deepest delight.

FOR OUR HEART OF STONE

We were born into the world with a disposition innately opposed to God. Spiritually, it's what Scripture describes as a "heart of stone"—cold, unyielding, lifeless. It's captivated by foolish thinking and controlled by wayward lusts, so that we're "alienated from the life of God." Our thoughts, delights, and pursuits are out of alignment with His.

It's actually worse than simply being neutral toward God. "Enmity against God," as Paul puts it, is in fact the very heartbeat of our flesh. Our natural, inbred response toward God and His commands is distaste, anger, and undeniable rebellion.

That's why God's New Covenant promise to His people

through the prophet Ezekiel was this: "I will give you *a new heart...*a heart *of flesh.*" To offset our natural heart of stone, this new heart is inclined and warm and responsive toward God and His righteousness—the kind of heart only God can give.

Earlier we faced the fact that God hasn't yet removed our old heart—our natural, sinful disposition. Even as we grow in Christ, that disposition can never be improved or reformed. There will never come a time when it loves, fears, or even tolerates God. At every turn our flesh despises Him, detests His rule, and yearns to do whatever He's forbidden. It obeys God only when it believes there will be greater personal benefit than if it disobeys. Till the day we die, it will be inclined toward levels of ungodliness that would cause us unspeakable shame if anyone knew what we were thinking.

Even while preaching and performing weddings, I've had thoughts that shocked me with their hideous wickedness. I used to think a time would come when I'd be free from that; I'm now convinced it will never happen in this lifetime. I'm seldom surprised anymore at the degradation my flesh can stoop to and the thoughts it's capable of. But when this happens I try to remind myself of three things.

First, it isn't the real me producing such thoughts; it's my flesh. And for my flesh, such thoughts are merely par for the course.

Second, the thought itself isn't sin, though my response to it can be. My responsibility is to not allow ungodly thoughts or temptation to find a welcome home within my soul.

Third, there's something I desire far more at the core of my being than the sinful thought or the temptation at hand. Although it often doesn't feel this way at the moment, I always have a supernatural set of godly inclinations that *do* want to go God's direction. And so do you.

Heart Etching

These inclinations are within us because of God's New Covenant promise for His people: "I will put My law in their minds, and write it on their hearts."

God hasn't altered His commands to fit our hearts; He has altered our hearts to fit His commands.

Describing this reality, Paul reminded the Corinthians that they were like an "epistle" or letter from Christ, in which the writing is "not on tablets of stone [as was true of the Old Covenant] but on tablets of flesh, that is, of *the heart.*" The Greek wording in this passage indicates a *permanent* etching within. And the place of that etching is our heart, the most central facet of our being. God went for the jugular, so to speak.

Paul also emphasized that this writing is supernatural—"not with ink but by the Spirit of the living God." Our new disposition is never separate from the Holy Spirit. Were the Holy Spirit to leave us, our new disposition would vanish in the same instant. Thank God for His assurance that this will never happen!

Deeper than our sin, deeper than our pain, deeper than our fears is something clean, pure, and godly within us that ceaselessly yearns to know and reflect God. The Lord, in effect, has made us liver lovers. We can do His will not only because it's good for us, but because it delights the taste buds of our new nature. The desire to do His will isn't something we have to work up, but something to fall back on.

NEVER A BURDEN

These new inclinations for doing God's will were given to you *before* the light of Scripture ever brought any aspect of God's will to your attention. James calls it "the implanted word," which he tells us to "receive with meekness." James is saying in essence, "Take hold of what you already have, that which is innate to your new nature." Ponder with your mind what God has already made your heart desire!

The birthright of every believer is an inner self that's supernaturally inscribed with the *whole* of Christ's teachings and commands—even to the extent that "we have the mind of Christ," as Scripture says.

Every command we come across in the Bible is therefore a vigorous reminder to do what we already desire. The Scriptures simply clarify in our minds what we already want to do in our regenerate heart.

This must have been what the apostle John had in mind when he wrote that God's commands "are not burdensome." (Though I appreciate the honesty of Francis Schaeffer who said that for years he refused to preach on this passage because he had no idea what it meant! My guess is that many Christians, if they were honest, would say the same.) Whatever John means here, it applies to all God's commands. He doesn't say that "some" or even "most" of God's commandments "are not burdensome."

What this means practically is that you'll never find a biblical command from God for which He hasn't already given you a desire to obey. Reading God's Word, we need never ask Him for the desire to do what we read; we thank Him for having already given us the desire, and ask Him to help us appropriate it meaningfully.

LOVE, FOR EXAMPLE

As an example of one of these instinctive biblical commands, take the instruction to "love one another."

Paul tells the Thessalonian believers, "Concerning brotherly love you have no need that I should write to you, for you yourselves are *taught by God* to love one another." Paul knows the Lord has already taken care of instructing them to love their fellow brethren. How did God do this? Not through external instruction, but through their internal desire.

I remember clearly experiencing this when I first became a believer. I was a high school senior at the time. Prior to my conversion I used to ridicule a group of "Jesus freak" students who held Bible studies on the steps of our high school at lunch. I joined my buddies in mocking them, saying, "Preach it, brother," and other things I now regret.

After I trusted Christ, the first time I passed by this group of Christian students, I sensed a fondness toward them that completely caught me off guard. It was as if I now was on their team, that we were somehow connected. Part of me (my flesh) couldn't believe this was happening; another part (my new disposition) couldn't deny the reality. Only years later did I realize from Scripture what had happened. Like the Thessalonians, I had been "taught by God" to love my fellow believers.

ANOTHER EXAMPLE: REMAINING SEXUALLY PURE

Another example of God's implanted Word is His command to remain sexually pure. Why should we obey this command? There are several good reasons, but one of the best, because of our new

disposition, is something we often overlook. At the deepest level of
our being, *we want to remain pure*. We want the joy of purity rather
than the counterfeit pleasure of illicit sexuality.

The only way to overcome our lower passions is to glut our
higher ones. Oswald Chambers reminds us, "Human nature, if it is
healthy, demands excitement. And if it does not obtain its thrilling
excitement in the right way, it will seek it in the wrong. God never
made bloodless stoics; He makes passionate saints."

This is why it's important, when facing temptation, to ask ourselves not "What do I want?" but "What do I *really* want?" What
do we as "passionate saints" desire at the deepest level of our being,
not merely at the surface?

No More Heart Change Needed

I once received a brochure advertising a significant conference on
ministry and leadership. As I opened it I noticed that one of the
scheduled keynote speakers was a man I'd gone to seminary with
and come to know fairly well.

I'd like to say my immediate response to seeing his name and
picture was excitement for the opportunity God had given him.
But that wasn't the case by a long shot. I found myself internally
jealous that he, not I, had been asked to speak. Then I felt guilty,
because he's a wonderful man of God who richly deserved to speak
at the conference.

As I began processing this before the Lord and confessing my
sin, I asked Him to change my heart toward this brother and his
ministry opportunity. Nothing seemed to happen. I began thinking of my past and present thought patterns and coping strategies

that contributed to this sinful jealousy, but this only made my mood darker.

Then God gently reminded me there was something deeper in me than this jealousy. I began dwelling on the reality that God had written His law on my heart, that according to the New Covenant reality at the deepest core of my being, I *was* excited for this brother.

I began to sense faint stirrings of genuine gratitude for my brother's ministry. As I continued in this reflection, a clear joy for him continued to escalate in my heart. It was a joy I could take no credit for whatsoever; it was an implanted joy that God had deposited in my heart at conversion.

Instead of asking God to change my heart in that situation, what helped me most was fully remembering that God has *already* granted me a changed heart through His Spirit and that what I need most is to appropriate it.

What Our New Heart Is Like

The new heart God has given us is one that's warm toward Him, a heart inflamed with delight and affection for the One who so marvelously redeemed us, a heart that's soft and compliant toward commands.

It's a heart that loves God, just as He promised: "And the LORD your God will circumcise your heart...to love the LORD your God." Love for God isn't something we're called to create, but to appropriate. Humbling as it may be to admit, none of us is born into this world with any genuine love toward God. Love for Him is the permanent, unshakable passion of the Holy Spirit within us. In other words, *we cannot love God unaided.*

Likewise, we cannot fear God unaided. Fearing Him is another gifted disposition granted to us at salvation. No one is born into the world with the ability to genuinely fear God. It must be given. Therefore God promises, "I will put My fear in their hearts so that they will not depart from Me."

How hopeful this is for those of us who feel we don't honor and reverence the Lord as we should! We don't have to manufacture a proper fear for Him, but simply appropriate the indwelling, divinely placed fear already there. Certainly we're called to nourish and stimulate this fear, as well as our love for Him, but we're never adding to what's there, only bringing its fullness to the surface.

Every aspect of our new disposition is something to be developed and nurtured, but it is and always will be the gift of God. We can never take credit for initiating any warmth toward God of any kind; it's provided through the Holy Spirit alone.

Even our heart to know God is a gift. "I will give them a heart to know Me," God promised as part of the New Covenant. These words from the book of Jeremiah have been of great spiritual help to me. When I feel dry and lifeless toward God, I remind myself of this reality. It isn't my responsibility to create a desire for knowing Him, but to fall back on the supernaturally implanted desire for knowing Him that was given me at conversion.

During times of spiritual dryness, I ask God to point out what competing desires are keeping my deepest desire submerged. Almost always it has to do with idolatry in some form—ministry success, material security, approval of others, or something else. As I confess these things and ask God to help me tap in to what He has placed within me, I normally sense the desire for knowing Him beginning to rise up.

Our Desires and Our Conscience

How is this new disposition different from our conscience, the basic sense of right and wrong that all human beings have? After all, Paul affirms that even unbelievers have "the work of the law written in their hearts."

But there's a distinction between "the *work* of the law" (or "the requirements of the law," as it's also translated) and the law itself. As Renald Showers explains in *The New Nature,* all unbelievers "have a moral consciousness, a sense of right and wrong, inherent within them," and this consciousness comes "as an inherent attribute of their total human nature."

But the New Covenant provides something totally different. When God actually writes His law in our hearts in the New Covenant sense, He makes His commands *instinctive* within us.

We see illustrations of a similar instinctiveness in nature. How do birds know exactly when and where to migrate for the winter? Do they take classes in southern migration? Obviously not. God has written His "migration law" on their hearts, so to speak. How did those same birds even learn to fly? It was because they followed a God-given instinct.

In the same way, righteousness, holiness, and love are the instinctive, innate desires of our new heart, now that we're reborn. While many times these new inclinations don't feel real, that doesn't mean they aren't real. They're temporarily in hiding, lurking beneath the surface of competing inclinations that *seem* more alive at the time. The starting point for moving forward is to remember that our godless inclinations are only a part of the picture; the whole picture includes clean, pure, joyous inclinations toward the will of God.

These inclinations will never leave you nor forsake you. At the deepest level of your being, *you always desire to do all the will of God*. There's never a time when you don't, never a situation where you don't. It certainly doesn't seem this way many times, but nonetheless it's true.

We must take it by faith. "The moment we believe God's promise and act upon it," J. Oswald Sanders writes, "we will find it true in experience."

STILL WONDERING?

You may still be wondering if this revolutionary view of our inner disposition is really true. You might confess that what you feel most deeply is actually an indifference toward God; perhaps while reading this chapter you've been trying to get in touch with more godly desires, but they seem to elude you.

Let me ask you a favor. Read Psalm 1 slowly (it's only six verses), seeking to quietly enjoy it. Then come back to this page.

Wasn't there something within you that stirred at the thought of becoming the tree mentioned in this Psalm? Didn't you find something deep within that was enticed by the prospect of "delighting" in God's Word and not just dutifully reading it?

Now let me ask you to do the same thing with Paul's prayer that begins in Ephesians 3:14. Read it slowly, quietly.

Again, wasn't there something deep within you that at least began to rise up in agreement with this prayer? Did the possibility of knowing "the love of Christ which passes knowledge" start to kindle an inclination at the core of your being for that very thing?

A final question: What words of praise from someone else do

you most long to hear? Can you imagine anything more thrilling than to hear Jesus tell you, "Well done, good and faithful servant.... Enter into the joy of your [L]ord"? By comparison, I'm sure your regenerate heart counts any earthly praise as nothing but vain flattery.

And *that,* my friend, *comes only from your new disposition.*

CHAPTER 10

Both Faith
and Feelings

The gladdest thing on earth is to have a real God.

R. A. TORREY

Tragically, too many Christians are almost wholly unaware of the new desires and disposition God has placed within them. We're told to "walk by faith and not by feelings." To avoid the mistake of living solely by emotions, we're encouraged just to do what is right, "and the feelings will follow."

All this is only partially true. The other side of the coin is that God has implanted within us a whole new set of desires, or "feelings," for us to make the most of. Emotions have been portrayed for too long as a hindrance to true godliness.

WHAT ABOUT EMOTIONS?

You may have figured out by now that I'm an admirer of Jonathan Edwards, who happens to be my fifth great-grandfather (which means I'm also related to Aaron Burr, one of American history's great scoundrels; you have to take the good with the bad!). What I admire most about Edwards isn't his intellect (perhaps unrivaled in American history), but his fervent passion and love for his

Redeemer. Typical of passages in his *Personal Narrative* is this one: "The sense I had of divine things would often of a sudden kindle up, as it were, a sweet burning in my heart, an ardour of soul that I know not how to express."

One of the most significant works produced by this brilliant and passionate man of God is titled *Religious Affections.* He wrote this book to correct an error in his day, one that many segments of today's evangelical church are facing as well. It's the dangerous misconception that emotions have little to no importance in true spirituality.

During the prosperous mid-eighteenth century in the New England colonies, most churches had settled into dead orthodoxy. Deep dependence on God was eroding. Bible truths were being taught, but often in a lifeless manner to congregations equally devoid of fervor.

The primary message from the pulpits was first, *Believe what is true,* and second, *Do what is right.* The combination of right beliefs and right behavior equaled true spirituality; emotions had little or nothing to do with it.

When God at this time used the ministry of Edwards to help bring about a revival known as the Great Awakening, it was opposed vigorously by many ministers and church leaders because of the emotional excesses and religious fanaticism it produced. Edwards responded to their criticism in *Religious Affections.*

He first distinguished between true and false religious affections. He acknowledged that some experiences were counterfeits in the flesh, but equally insisted that others were the result of God's Spirit.

Edwards also made the bold assertion that true Christian living consists "in large part" of true "holy affections." It isn't enough, he taught, to know and to do what is right; a Christian is also to "*experience* what is divine" on the level of the emotions and feelings. The Christian life, Edwards wrote, "contains things too great for us to be lukewarm." True Christianity "is *always a dynamic thing.* Its power is in the inward exercises of the heart."

Edwards's contention (which I believe is thoroughly biblical) is that, at a very fundamental level, it's impossible *not* to live by feelings. Every decision we face, every action we're called on to take, is accompanied by a sense of either like or dislike—our affections, in other words. These affections, he explained, will motivate us either to accept and pursue that action or to oppose and turn away from it.

These affections or emotions can, of course, deceive and lead us astray; that's why God's revealed truth must always remain the final arbiter of what we do. But these same emotions can also help propel us toward greater godliness and devotion. The right approach isn't to demean or dismiss emotions altogether, but to utilize them fully in the purposes for which God gave them.

The true religious affections Edwards spoke of are in essence the new disposition God has given us through the New Covenant. If God has so mightily provided this new disposition for us, in all its emotional aspects, certainly He must want us to fully avail ourselves of it.

DUTY OR DESIRE?

Many times we approach the desire for God's will as either something we must work up or something that really doesn't matter so long as we *do* what's right. Certainly we should always do what's right, whether or not we feel so inclined. But God has seen to it that we're internally resourced with dependable, divinely implanted affections that make doing His will more of a spiritual outing than a spiritual chore.

Think of it from God's point of view. Suppose I were to come home one day with a bouquet of the finest red roses for my wife, and after she thanked me I responded, "You're welcome, Sandy—I'm only doing my duty as your husband."

How would she feel? Not very warmed, I can assure you. When we come before God with our bouquet of dry, dutiful obedience, it's the same for Him.

It isn't just obedience God is after; it's a certain kind of obedience: "Serve the LORD with *gladness*." "These things I have spoken to you," Jesus said, "that your *joy* may be full." The kind of obedience that brings pleasure to God's heart and glory to God's name is the glad-hearted, voluntary offering of grace-soaked saints. It's a glad-heartedness that ultimately can come only from God Himself through His gift of our new disposition.

This is one of the most liberating truths I know of in Christianity. I've spent so many years trying to muster up the desire for what I knew God was requiring of me, or praying that God would change my heart. The good news of sanctification is that *God has already changed* my heart, and yours as well. Our role now is to fall back in faith on the unalterable change God made within us at conversion—a disposition shot through with godly affections from the Holy Spirit.

This God-intentioned desire is why the believer living in sin is really the most miserable creature on earth. He can't get the divine bent of his soul taken away, yet that bent robs him of the ability to fully enjoy sin. He can't escape knowing at the deepest level of his being that he was made for God, that his rebellion against righteousness is really kicking against the goads.

On the other hand, living as an outright disciple of Christ is the greatest favor a believer can do himself. When is an eagle most satisfied—in a cage or out in nature? Obviously out in nature, because eagles were created by God for such soaring freedom. Likewise no believer can be fully satisfied while caged in sin. Each of us was made to soar, to feel the currents of God's righteousness lifting us to ever-increasing heights of godliness.

Unrestrained Indulgence

The New Covenant doesn't mean any kind of downgrade in obeying God. His commands are not suggestions, helpful hints, or practical advice; they're royal decrees, the King's rightful demands upon His subjects. To disregard or disobey them will always be high treason against heaven. But in the New Covenant, God has also provided a new, internal appetite for knowing and doing these same decrees.

God has turned the "have tos" into "want tos." He has caused His unwavering commands to become an inbred *delight* to our new nature.

I don't believe *delight* is too strong a word to describe the depth of pleasure our new disposition holds for God's standards. For every command He gives, He has infused within us a vigorous, holy inclination toward keeping it.

This is why Jesus said, "My food is to do the will of Him who sent Me, and to finish His work." He knew that doing God's will brought strength and vigor to His soul, which is always the case when divine disposition connects with divine will.

In a section of Romans where Paul depicts his own struggle between obedience and sin, he describes himself as "one who wills [literally "desires"] to do good." He saw himself as someone who fundamentally wanted to do God's will. In his "inward man," Paul insisted, "I delight in the law of God." The Greek word here for "delight" is quite strong; from its root we derive our word *hedonism*. And what is this "inward man" Paul speaks of? It's the new Paul, the real Paul.

That, my friend, is the new you as well. Your essential identity is that of desiring to do God's will. You can't help it; that's how God rewired you at your new birth. At the deepest core of our being, you and I "delight in the law of God." Our inner man and the law of God are never at odds; rather, our new disposition hedonistically enjoys the deep and holy pleasure of being united with God and His ways.

That's why *true obedience is the unrestrained indulgence of our new nature.* Obedience to God isn't just denying our flesh, though that will always be involved. It's also satisfying our new, divinely bestowed appetite for godliness. God calls us to a life of shamelessly glutting this new nature with the delicacies of Spirit-wrought obedience.

This is why James describes the Word of God as "the law of liberty." God's commands are designed not to enslave us, but to free us to experience what we were redeemed for. "He who looks into the perfect law of liberty and continues in it, and is not a forgetful hearer but a doer of the work, *this one will be blessed in what he* does [literally, "in the doing"]." The word here for "blessed" speaks of an interior, supernatural joy. It's the joy of glutting our new nature.

SPIRITUAL CONNECTORS FOR SPIRITUAL INDULGENCE

There's nothing in the New Covenant that validates or encourages us to neglect what are commonly referred to as "spiritual disciplines"—such things as prayer, fasting, Bible study, and Scripture memorization. *"Exercise yourself* toward godliness," Paul commanded Timothy, and we need that exercise as well. There's no inherent legalism whatsoever in doing these things.

I prefer the term "spiritual connectors" for these practices, because they're necessary for connecting us with the presence of God in spiritually enriching ways. Each one is indeed a discipline in the sense that our flesh always opposes them, but each is meant also to satisfy the deepest hunger of our new disposition—for knowing God in all His ravishing fullness. *Every spiritual discipline is at the same time a spiritual indulgence.* Through these spiritual connectors, God is calling us to satiate our souls with the only commodity that can fully satisfy them.

That's why when these things are done mechanically or to impress others or to obligate God to bless us, they lose all meaning. They become nothing more than "shoulds." But praying, studying, meditating, and memorizing will always be "want tos" when we exercise them with a view to God's glory, in dependence on His Spirit, and for the delight of knowing Him more intimately.

Enjoying God's Word, Prayer, and Witnessing

Does a newborn infant need a commandment to long for his mother's milk? Hardly. And this is the very image Peter gives of our partaking of Scripture—"As newborn babes, desire the pure milk of the word." It's a command simply to do what is innately instinctive to us. We're to feast regularly on the Word of God for the same reason we eat—because we want to! God has placed an appetite within our hearts that cannot be satisfied with anything less than the bread, meat, and honey of God's Word.

The same is true for prayer. When Paul commands us to pray "in the Spirit," "with all perseverance and supplication," he's telling us to merely cooperate with what the Spirit within us is already doing and has made us want to do. Prayer is the essential way we eagerly accept Scripture's warm invitation to "draw near" to God. Prayer's purpose, Oswald Chambers said, "is that we get ahold of God, not of the answer." "Prayer," wrote R. A. Torrey, "makes God real." "True prayer," wrote Samuel Zwemer, "is God the Holy Spirit talking to God the Father in the name of God the Son, and the believer's heart is the prayer room."

Present also within us is an inherent desire for evangelism. As scary as sharing our faith can be, it's the innate yearning of our new heart. We were born to reproduce. There's an incomparable depth of joy and exhilaration of spirit awaiting every believer in the high adventure of warring on behalf of God's kingdom. Charles Spurgeon identified a "perfect, overflowing, unutterable happiness of the purest and most enabling order" that he never knew until helping others find the Savior.

The good news about our new disposition is one of the most joyous and liberating truths in Christianity; it's also one of the best hidden. I've no doubt Satan wants to keep it this way because of the tremendous damage it would do to his kingdom. When God's people reach deep within and realize that evangelism is something they *want* to do, not just *should* do, the impact may be staggering.

SEEING OTHERS REALISTICALLY

Because of the New Covenant we can say with Paul, "From now on, we regard no one according to the flesh." Instead we can view all other believers with this radical assumption: *They desire to do the will of God.*

In the New Testament, no group of believers showed less tangible evidence of being newly created in Christ than those in Corinth. Yet Paul affirmed to them that the Spirit of God had engraved God's law upon their hearts, and with clear confidence he wrote more about New Covenant realities to them than to any other church. Where did this confidence come from? "Through Christ toward God," he said. Paul knew the Corinthians were participants in the New Covenant not primarily because of visible fruit in their lives, but because of the certainty of Christ's abiding work in their hearts.

If our children are believers, we can have the same confidence about them. Deep down they want to do the will of God, hard as this is to believe sometimes. We need to continually affirm the reality of their new disposition along with any correction of their fleshly living. We can do this with statements such as "I know you really want to be a person of integrity" or through asking questions that speak to their new heart, such as "What do you really want?" or "Did that feel good deep down?"

The Old Covenant approach to all these things is to emphasize *only* the "should," then add the exhortation to "do what is right." The way of the New Covenant is to point out the "want to" along with the "should," then emphasize the deep joy of glorifying God through doing what is right by the power of God.

This is why I no longer see preaching and teaching as an attempt to convict and challenge Christians to do what they have no real desire for. Instead my role is to coax to the surface their deepest longing, while also exposing the foolishness and perversity of living contrary to their divine design.

Are you experiencing in a rich way your own God-given desires for knowing and obeying Him? Is it possible you're out of balance in any aspects of duty versus desire? If so, in what way?

How would you describe your present understanding and experience of spiritual disciplines—our spiritual connectors to God? What would it mean for you to exercise them with more of a view to God's glory, in more dependence on His Spirit, and with more delight in His intimacy?

As you relate to other believers around you, are you consciously remembering that a fundamental desire for God is their deepest emotional reality?

As we prepare to move on to the last of our four major New Covenant provisions, ponder the prayerful longings for God in Psalms 63 and 84. Then thank God that He has made them your own.

Releasing Your New Power

*New Testament Christianity is not just a formal, polite, correct,
and orthodox kind of faith and belief. No! What characterizes it is
this element of love and passion, this pneumatic element,
this life, this vigour, this abandon, this exuberance.*

D .   M A R T Y N   L L O Y D - J O N E S

May I confess a fantasy of mine? I've always wanted to fly. Without
an airplane, that is. I know it's neurotic, but I can't help it. I've even
had dreams where I was floating, even soaring, just using my own
two arms. It was great, and waking up was a disappointment.

But no matter how much I might like to fly there's obviously
no way it's going to happen. My "want to" isn't connected with the
resources necessary to make flying a "can do." My only hope is that
there really are wings for us in heaven.

In the same way, it isn't enough simply to *want* to do God's
will. Our best intentions and highest resolves are still impotent to
overcome our flesh's downward pull. To put it another way:

New Purity + New Identity + New Disposition
= frustration and defeat

Only when the provision of *New Power* is added to the equa-
tion does genuine victory become possible.

Tell Them 'Ow

Scottish philosopher Thomas Carlyle was once sitting around the family fire, chatting with his parents about church and preachers. "Well, I will tell you one thing," he boldly asserted. "If I were ever to preach, I'd make short work of it. I would go up to the pulpit, look out on the congregation, and tell them this: 'You good people know what you should be doing. Now go home and do it!'"

After a pause, Carlyle's mother, a godly saint, looked him in the eyes and responded, "Aye, Thomas, but would ye tell them 'ow? Would ye tell them 'ow?"

Isn't this the great question facing each of us? Not *what* we should be doing, but *how* to do it. How do we find the power to carry out what God has made us want to do through our new disposition?

God has given us the answer through the New Covenant: "I will put My Spirit within you and cause you to walk in My statutes." God gives us a new "can do" through His Spirit to carry out the new "want tos" of our new disposition. Only *God* can fulfill through us what *God* has inclined within us.

This new power from God's Spirit is the same power that raised Christ from the dead. It is also the new power that *alone* can resurrect us from the defeated, death-like quality of life to which our flesh seeks to hold us in bondage.

Skis, but No Boat

No matter how much we *want* to obey them, God's standards for us as outlined in His Word can never *in themselves* infuse life-giving power. In fact, they actually breed death in the flesh. As we've seen, law agitates the flesh, stimulates sin, provokes guilt, and thunders forth condemnation—in short, "the letter kills," as Paul said. I've found in my own life that when I view obedience to one of God's commands only as a "should," an internal resistance and deadness toward that very command tends to set in immediately.

Only resurrection power can lift this burden and provide the rest of soul Jesus promises. And this life-giving power is found only in a *Person,* not in precepts. "The letter kills, but *the Spirit* gives life."

Whenever the shoulds of the Christian life have become our central focus, we revert to living under a code (the letter) rather then through a Person (the Spirit). When we feel the legitimate command of God hammering down apart from supernatural provision, we droop under such unbearable weight.

It's like being in a lake with water skis but with no motorboat. The skis offer direction and stability (as the law does), but they cannot, of themselves, keep you skimming over the waters. They can't even keep you from sinking.

Only Christ's resurrection power, the new power of the New Covenant, can keep us from sinking into the dark waters of death-like living, so that we instead arise and move forward in the glorious adventure of supernatural living.

WANTING A PIECE OF THE ACTION

What keeps us from supernaturally moving forward more often?

You'll recall our earlier "what-why-how" requirements for something to qualify as good from God's perspective: It must be done *in accordance with the standard of God, for the glory of God,* and *through the Spirit of God.*

We have no chance of ever accomplishing such requirements *in our natural state*. This is why Paul admonishes the Galatians, "Are you so foolish? Having begun in the Spirit, are you now being made perfect by the flesh?" To think our spiritual growth can be empowered by that which is innately hostile to God—our flesh—is not only wrong, it's lunacy.

Yet it's so hard to yield fully to this truth. Our flesh so desperately wants in on the action. It yearns to get at least partial credit for the good in our lives. It strives for at least some control and violently protests the terrifying prospect of relying only on God.

You see, our problem isn't in *trusting* God; it's in trusting God *alone*. We want to know His help is there when we've run out of options, but our flesh can't bear the thought of His being our only option.

A WALKING CIVIL WAR

In his letter to the Romans, we find Paul caught in the throes of wanting to live for God but being dragged away by the power of his flesh: "For what I am doing, I do not understand. For what I will to do, that I do not practice; but what I hate, that I do."

Paul was a walking civil war, caught between the pull of his flesh and the tug of his new nature. Words like *frustrated, overwhelmed, hopeless, restless,* and *guilt-ridden* are all a fair description of his Christian experience here—and perhaps they describe your Christian experience now as well.

Is this the normal Christian life? The answer is both yes and no.

The answer is yes in that all this is clearly normative. There will never come a time when you and I are not a walking civil war to some degree. "For the flesh lusts against the Spirit, and the Spirit against the flesh; and these are contrary to one another, so that you do not do the things that you wish." Until heaven, our battle against the flesh will never cease.

In another sense the answer is an emphatic no. God never intended His children to resign themselves to spiritual defeat as a way of life. "Thanks be to God who always leads us in triumph *in Christ.*" God, who provided His Son to remove the penalty of our sins, also provides His Son to defeat the pressing power of our sins. While the reality of our war with sin will never cease, the intensity of that battle is dramatically affected by how fully we appropriate the provision of the New Covenant, especially our new power.

We access this power of Christ through the Holy Spirit within. Therefore Paul exhorts us, "Walk in the Spirit, and you shall not fulfill the lust of the flesh." He didn't say that by walking in the Spirit we wouldn't *experience* the lust of the flesh; rather, we won't fulfill those lusts if we rely on the Spirit's resurrection power.

But until we become convinced to the core of our being that only Christ Himself provides the power for godliness, we'll continue to thwart His ministry within us by unwittingly depending on our flesh.

EMBRACING INADEQUACY

Because my father died when I was young, there were many things I never learned growing up, including basic tasks like house repairs and car maintenance.

One of the most important skills I failed to pick up was leadership. As a result, I've spent most of my life running from it. Frankly,

I find leadership—whether at home or church—to be scary. A part of me would love to always follow and let someone else take the risks. But God hasn't seen fit to allow this. For whatever reason, He's placed me in many situations requiring me to lead.

What has helped me in leadership more than anything else has been learning to embrace my inadequacy. (It's one thing to admit inadequacy; it's a very different thing to embrace it.) When a difficult decision must be made or a hard situation handled, I'm helped most by going before the Lord and saying something like…

"Lord, I don't have a clue what to do here. I'm fearful and would love to not be in this situation. Heaven looks really good now, and this would be a great time for You to come back.

"But if that can't be, then I need You to take me through this every step of the way. I have nothing to offer of my own ingenuity or strength; I need your wisdom and power as badly as I need the air I breathe.

"As I move forward, help me do so with desperate dependence upon You every second. I joyously and unreservedly confess that I'm not a leader, I'm not able to handle this situation on my own, and any good must come solely through You. I simply ask You now to flow through me, Lord Jesus, and help me stay out of Your way."

Unless I begin by embracing my inadequacy in this way, I end up either leading in my flesh or backing away altogether.

Who, Not What

Another word to describe this embracing of inadequacy is *brokenness*. What I mean by brokenness isn't primarily anguish of heart (though that, too, may be present), but absence of self-confidence.

It's tossing overboard all hope of producing anything good on our own. Until Paul could say with heartfelt conviction, "For I know that in me (that is, in my flesh) *nothing good dwells,*" he remained too strong for God to be able to help.

We must come to the absolute end of our spiritual rope. As long as we call out, "O weak man that I am, I need help to make it," we're still too strong for God's power to fully intervene in our lives. We'll be ready for Christ to start moving us forward toward victory only when we cry out in despair, as Paul did: "O wretched man that I am! Who will deliver me from this body of death?"

That means turning for help in the right direction, as Paul did, and not reaching for a counterfeit rope that can't do the job. Paul didn't ask, "*What* will deliver me?" but "*Who* will deliver me?" He then gave the answer: "I thank God—through *Jesus Christ our Lord!*" Only the indwelling Christ can overcome the downward pull of sin's power in our flesh.

Tragically, most sanctification systems pursued by Christians today are based on a "what"—spiritual disciplines, counseling, Christian service, and so on. These can be helpful in leading us to the "Who," but they're impotent in themselves to deliver us from sin's power.

Until we ruthlessly shed all hope and confidence in our own ability to carry out God's will, no amount of sound Bible teaching on the subject will make any practical difference in our lives. That's why many of us need a kind of reconversion in which we come to Christ for sanctification with the same desperate dependence we had when we came to Him for salvation. Or in the words of Paul, "*As* you therefore have received Christ Jesus the Lord, *so walk in Him.*" Continue just the way you began—utterly needy, radically dependent.

AN IMPORTANT BALANCE

Continuing in Christ in this way will mean maintaining an important balance that often is neglected.

If we focus only on our new provisions through the New Covenant without properly taking into account our fallen, earthly nature, unwarranted optimism will result. We'll fail to appropriately recognize our human depravity and the inescapable reality of struggle.

But if we focus only on our fallen nature without properly taking into account our new provisions, it will cause unwarranted resignation. We'll fail to utilize our divine resources and remain stuck at a needlessly low level of spirituality.

The great present hope for the believer is something Paul reminds us of when he says that God is "working continuously in you so that you both *desire* and *do* the Father's good pleasure." This assertion points both to our new disposition and our new power. There's never a time when God provides the power to do His will without also providing the desire; nor does He ever provide the desire without the power. God provides supernaturally both the yearning to do His will and the ability to accomplish it, but we must appropriate both by faith.

EMPOWERMENT FOR IMPACT

As we draw upon this new power, in radical dependence on the Holy Spirit's presence, what will it mean for us?

Among other things, it will enable us to reflect His Son to others and to advance His kingdom purposes in this world. Jesus foretold what His disciples would become through the Holy Spirit's power: "You shall be witnesses to Me...to the end of the earth." He calls His followers to make converts and to present these converts "complete in Christ." *Christ is calling you and me and every believer to a life that furthers the gospel's worldwide penetration* as well as an in-depth cultivation of that gospel in those who respond.

Does that seem impossible? It should. Mark this: *God will never call you to something you can do.* Period. If you can do what God has called you to *without* the new power God alone provides...*then you missed what God has called you to.* God calls us only to that which requires Him.

This is why Paul exclaimed with genuine humility that he dared not speak of anything except what Christ had accomplished through him. Reliance on Christ was the secret behind Paul's impact on the world of his day; it's also the secret behind *our* impact on the world of our day.

ENLIGHTENMENT

Dependence on God is also critical for opening us to the Spirit's ministry of inward enlightening. This is a God-wrought illumination that enables us to understand spiritual truth beyond a merely intellectual level. D. L. Moody used to say that the Bible without the Holy Spirit is like "a sundial by moonlight." It takes God's Spirit to spiritually comprehend the words He Himself authored. That's why it's so important for us to read God's Word in childlike dependence on the Spirit, permeating our reading and meditation with prayer.

The Spirit also enlightens us to the excellencies and beauty of Christ. He takes the Lord's radiant realities and reveals them to our hearts with supernatural vividness so that we actually see "the light of the knowledge of the glory of God in the face of Jesus Christ."

The Spirit of God also enlightens us concerning sins in our life. Ultimately all sin occurs because of a breakdown in our relationship with Christ. Whenever an act of sin is present in our life, deep reliance on Christ is absent. The Holy Spirit loves us too much and is too jealous for God's glory to allow such sin to go unexposed. He may convict us through other people, through His Word, or simply through His own quiet, piercing work in our souls.

In the apostle John's terminology, sin takes place only when "abiding" stops: "Whoever abides in Him does not sin." Whatever *abiding* means (we'll explore it more later), it's such a profoundly powerful undertaking that it's impossible to be genuinely engaged in it and be sinning at the same time.

Meanwhile, let me ask you: Are you learning to fully embrace your inadequacy so that you can fully rely on the new power that is God's gift to you? In your Christian growth, are you depending upon anything in your life other than the Holy Spirit's power? And what is it that God has specifically called you to in your life that can be fulfilled only by Himself?

As you think about these things, observe in Romans 8 how the provisions of our new purity, our new identity, our new disposition, and our new power work together.

CHAPTER 12

Dynamic Dependence

The Spirit is an imperative necessity.
Only the Eternal Spirit can do eternal deeds.

A. W. TOZER

Let me ask you a hard question, the answer to which has everything to do with understanding the vital significance of our new power.

Here it is. If you had to choose between having Jesus at your side or the Holy Spirit in your heart, which would you choose?

Think about it: Christ physically at your side, actually telling you what to do and showing you how, or the Holy Spirit, invisibly, mystically residing within the deep recesses of your heart. Any way you slice it, it's not an easy choice.

The reality is that Christ has already made the choice for you. It's found in His words to His disciples: "It is to your advantage that I go away; for if I do not go away, the Helper [the Holy Spirit] will not come to you; but if I depart, I will send Him to you." Why would Christ say that His own exit and the Holy Spirit's entrance would be to our advantage?

Imagine taking basketball lessons from Michael Jordan. He demonstrates exactly how to shoot, dunk, dribble, and steal. He patiently instructs you on all the game's intricacies. With all that great training and modeling, would you be able to play basketball like MJ? Obviously not.

But suppose there was a way Michael could mystically assimilate himself inside you, so that your body became his suit of clothes? He could leap through you, shoot through you, dunk through you. It would no longer be you playing basketball, but Jordan playing through you.

Sound familiar? "It is no longer I who live, but Christ lives in me." The normal Christian life is not our living for Christ, but Christ's living through us. Our body becomes His suit of clothes so that He loves through us, worships through us, witnesses through us, prays through us, and flows through us purely and powerfully. He does this through the Spirit, whom Jesus portrayed as "rivers [literally, "floods"] of living water" flowing from the heart of everyone believing in Him. The indwelling Spirit of God produces the outflowing life that God requires of us.

How then do we go about opening the floodgates of our lives so these rivers can spill forth unhindered?

A Picture to Think About

Perhaps the most instructive passage in Scripture for appropriating our new power is the picture Christ gave of the vine and its fruit-producing branches. "Abide in Me, and I in you," Jesus said as He gave the picture. "Without Me you can do nothing."

The vine, He says, is Himself, and we're the branches. But what exactly is it that we can't do without Him?

Jesus gives the answer: "Bear fruit." Without abiding in Him, we cannot fulfill the very design for which we were created. There are, of course, many things we can blatantly do without Christ, as well as many that we can do *for* Christ but in the flesh. Anything of lasting value, however, can only be done *through* Christ, by abiding in Him.

Clearly abiding is something more than just believing. But nowhere in Scripture does God give us a detailed analysis of the various components of abiding. If He did, I'm certain we would turn it into a formula rather than leaving it as it is—a pathway to vital relationship.

Instead, the Lord directs our attention to a vine with branches and tells us to meditate on the deeper spiritual realities conveyed by it, then commands us to go and do likewise. "I am the vine, you are the branches."

For our life in Christ, let me suggest three significant lessons to learn from the branch abiding in the vine.

CLOSE CONNECTION

A vine and its branch know no distance from each other; they're tightly connected, with no gaps. In the same manner, we're to maintain a close connection with the Lord, closing any known gaps in our relationship.

Unconfessed sin can create such a gap. If keeping our pride intact is more valuable than enjoying God's presence, we'll refuse to confess our sin honestly and humbly.

An unforgiving spirit can bring about a gap. Jesus said, "If you do not forgive men their trespasses, neither will your Father forgive your trespasses." These words have nothing to do with our eternal salvation but everything to do with our present experience of God.

Gaps in that experience result also from our having knowingly offended another believer without seeking to make it right. "Leave your gift there before the altar," Jesus says to anyone conscious of an unreconciled relationship yet seeking to approach God. "Go your way. First be reconciled to your brother, and then come and offer your gift." This doesn't mean every brother or sister will be willing to reconcile, but we'll have done our part. The gap between the Lord and us will be closed.

Besides closing such gaps, Jesus alludes to two primary ways for strengthening our connection with Him: "If you abide in Me, and *My words* abide in you, you will *ask* what you desire." Prayer and immersing ourselves in God's Word are both intensely relational. Both are meant to lead us ever deeper into the Lord's presence; both are absolute musts for genuine abiding.

DRAWING LIFE

The branch is continually and entirely dependent on the vine for vitality and support. Alone, it brings nothing to the fruit-bearing enterprise; all the good it accomplishes is drawn from the life-giving sap of the vine.

Jesus Himself lived the most dynamic life ever because He maintained the most dependent life ever. "The Son can do nothing of Himself," He declared. His example shouts from the mountain-tops that, like Him, we are as dependent on God for our spiritual life as we are on the air we breathe for our physical life.

What's the primary reason unbelievers don't come to Christ for salvation? They don't recognize their need. What's the primary reason believers don't come to Christ for sanctification? Exactly the same—we don't genuinely recognize our need.

"Apart from Me you can do *nothing*"—those words have not a trace of exaggeration to them. Yet our flesh tries to keep the prideful hope alive of accomplishing something worthy on our own. Usually we try it in areas that we consider our strengths: our intellect, our personal discipline, our godly upbringing (if we were so blessed), our personality traits, or our Christian training or education.

But the best intellect can never replace or even slightly lessen one's desperate need for the Holy Spirit's light. When we read our Bibles without bothering to ask for His enlightening, when we make plans and decisions without genuinely waiting to hear from God, we prove our conviction that unaided intellect is all we need.

A genuinely Christian home can teach and show the way of life, but it does absolutely nothing for flesh improvement. It can train a child to be religiously refined and socially respectable, but that same child's flesh is still as utterly vile and allergic to true good as that of someone growing up on the streets. Our flesh may accommodate itself to whatever Christian culture it's been placed within, and it may never seek satisfaction through drugs or illicit sexuality, but not even a perfect upbringing can infuse it with such goodness that the Holy Spirit becomes any less essential.

Personal discipline or willpower originating from the flesh is typically rigid, relationally distant, and quietly smug in its own achievements. But self-control as a fruit of the Spirit is relaxed, relationally enhancing, and humbly rejoicing in what God has enabled.

Just as personal discipline can be a counterfeit of the self-control that is a fruit of the Spirit, so it is with any of our perceived personality strengths. Charm and empathy can be counterfeits for love, cheerfulness for joy, steadiness for peace. Obviously there's nothing wrong with personality—God grants one to all of us. But it can subtly become our primary object of reliance in our relationships, leaving the Holy Spirit alone at the dance.

Even Christian education and ministry training can draw us away from desperate dependence. It's very tempting to fall back on them rather than the Lord Himself. Christian training can provide very helpful tools for ministry, but it can never provide strength for it.

Recently I was asked to meet with the parents of a college student who had just been killed. Before the meeting I kept asking myself, *What should I say in this situation?* There's nothing wrong with that question, but internally I was tense and insecure because I really had no answer. Subtly, I was seeking to fall back on ministry skills rather than on Christ Himself. My soul found no rest until I sensed the Lord assuring me that He would tell me what to say, but not until I got there. My primary responsibility was to love this mother and father out of my new heart, with the strength God would give me at that moment.

As it turned out the Lord didn't give me many words for them. But He did give me what I believe they needed most at the time: tears in my eyes and an arm around their shoulders.

A Divine Drunkenness

The branch remains fully open to the life of the vine flowing through it, quietly yielding to that which sustains its very existence. Only this produces fruit.

In another picture of this process, Paul says, "Do not be drunk with wine…but be filled with the Spirit." The best way to understand what *being filled* means here is to look at what it's contrasted with—drunkenness. What is Paul trying to illustrate through this seemingly offensive metaphor?

Controlled might be the best word for it. When someone is drunk, he's being controlled by alcohol, dominated by something foreign to him. Consequently he does that which, when sober, he would never do. Being filled with the Spirit essentially means being yielded to a foreign influence—heaven's divine intoxicant, the Holy Spirit, who causes us to be inebriated with the Person of Christ and His glory so that we do things that are foreign to our natural being.

This yieldedness to the Holy Spirit's control requires submission to His direction. Paul speaks of being "led by the Spirit of God." The Spirit is *on the move.* Our responsibility is to move with the movement.

ACTIVE PASSIVITY

Appropriating our new power comes through what Francis Schaeffer aptly termed "active passivity." This, it seems to me, is exactly what abiding is all about. We have an active part to play. We're commanded to do something—abide. Yet, paradoxically, accompanying our activity there must be a passivity, a radical, diligent dependence.

Years ago, when I was a tennis instructor, a woman asked me to give lessons to her two sons. Needing the money, I gladly agreed, not bothering to ask their ages. The next day she brought her two sons, ages five and six. Each of them was holding an adult-sized racket. I could tell immediately we were in trouble.

After showing them how to grip and swing their rackets, I began tossing balls to them. Each in his turn completely missed the ball. By the time the boys were getting their racket around, the ball had hit the backstop. We were going downhill in a hurry.

Then I asked a friend to toss the balls while I stood behind each boy, putting my hand over theirs as they gripped the racket. I told them to relax and I would hit the ball for them. As long as they relaxed in my strength, I was able to hit the ball over the net with them.

Then one boy said, "Okay, I can do it now." I stepped back and let him—and the results were disastrous. He asked if I would help him again, and I agreed. But this time, instead of fully relaxing in my strength and skill, he tried to help me. And as long as he was tensed up from trying to partially do it himself, I wasn't able to hit the ball over. He was too strong for me to work through him.

Finally he relaxed. Only then were we able to hit the ball again over the net. The secret? The little guy had to maintain close connection, desperate dependence, and utter yieldedness to me. He couldn't do it apart from me, nor could he do it by helping me; he merely cooperated with my working through Him. In a word, he was abiding.

The essence of abiding is that we fully cooperate with a Life not our own to bring forth fruit not our own. True godly character—"the fruit of the Spirit"—is the greatest evidence on earth of God's miracle-working power. God is most fully glorified through the ongoing radiance of a God-intoxicated life. And because of the presence of this new power in other believers' lives, I must view each one of them as a miracle awaiting greater unfolding.

How can you more fully tap into this new power in your own life? What are the possible gaps that need closing in your own intimacy with the Lord? And how can you allow the reality of this new power to influence the way you view other believers?

Meditate on Jesus' words in John 15 to help you embrace more closely your dependence on Him.

A Fresh Look at Intimacy with God

What fire is this that warms my soul?... O fire that burns forever,
and never dies, kindle me! O light which shines eternally, and never darkens,
illumine me!... How sweetly do you burn!

AUGUSTINE

My boyhood idol was an Australian tennis great named Roy Emerson. Until Pete Sampras recently surpassed him, Emerson held the record for the most grand slam championships in tennis history. As someone whose life was dominated by tennis, I read everything I could about Emerson. I watched him on television and tried—not very successfully—to model my own tennis game after his. I knew all kinds of interesting tidbits about him. I would have given anything to meet him, but there was little chance.

All this changed in the spring of 1974. Through a strange set of circumstances, I was hired to work for Emerson at a tennis resort for several weeks. I still remember the thrill and nervousness of finally getting to meet him and the pleasure of discovering how warm-hearted, accepting, and encouraging he was in person.

In the following weeks I was privileged to spend a good amount of time with him. Besides working under him giving tennis lessons, we were together often to eat, work out, and occasionally play golf. He invited me to play some exhibition tennis matches with him and really helped me with my game.

That broad grin I'd seen on his face in tennis magazines was even broader in person, especially when he pushed me beyond exhaustion. I'd often read about his feared backhand volley; now I discovered personally why it was revered.

Unexpectedly, he took a sincere interest in me, for which I'll always be grateful. He kindly answered my frequent questions about the places and events in the tennis world he had experienced.

It was all a dream come true beyond anything I could have imagined growing up.

I learned a very important lesson that spring. It's one thing to know *about* a person; it's a very, very different thing to come to know that individual personally.

To Feel the Fire

Nowhere is this more true than when it comes to knowing God.

How incomprehensible it is that God—the infinitely great God who is from everlasting to everlasting—passionately invites us not just to know about Him, but to know Him firsthand! He beckons us to gaze upon His excellence and beauty, to hear His voice, and to feel His touch within our souls. "He meant us to see Him," wrote A. W. Tozer, "and live with Him and draw our life from His smile."

It's one thing to know theological categories describing God's attributes; it's a very different thing to experience those attributes firsthand. Knowing God does involve an intellectual grasp of the truths of His being and His will, but it's much, much more. It's possible to gain a handle on the Word of God through diligent study and meticulous thought, yet fail to significantly experience within our soul the fire of the Spirit of Him to whom the Scriptures point.

How would you explain the taste of Coca-Cola to those who've never tasted anything like it? What would you liken it to so that they could fully understand? It's impossible. To truly know its taste, they must drink it. To know God, we must taste Him. As an old Scottish saying puts it, "Some things are better felt than telt." Unless we know God's fiery presence in our souls, we can be scholars but never worshipers.

All from Above

One of the most alluring promises in the New Covenant is this: "No more shall every man teach his neighbor, and every man his brother, saying, 'Know the LORD,' for *they all shall know Me,* from the least of them to the greatest of them, says the LORD."

Under the Old Covenant, God's people were called to "know the LORD" just as we are today. But only select individuals (normally prophets, priests, or kings) were granted significantly close access to God. Others had to go to a priest or elder for instruction—or to the written law itself. It always required an external source.

All this changes with the New Covenant. Every believer has as much access to God and His wisdom as any other believer. God isn't one iota more disposed to let Himself be known by Billy

Graham than by you or me. His door is never closed to us while He meets with someone more important.

He delights to reveal His eternal wisdom to your seeking heart and His ravishing splendor to your soul. He does all this through the internal medium of His Holy Spirit (though external sources are often the instruments through which He works).

God Himself does this for us because *it requires God to know God.* How crucial it is to recognize that we cannot gain any knowledge of God, or learn anything of eternal significance, through our own efforts alone. True spiritual understanding will never occur until it's given from above through the Holy Spirit.

"Blessed are you," Jesus once said to Peter, "for flesh and blood has not revealed this to you, but My Father who is in heaven." Subjects like science, mathematics, philosophy, and history require only "flesh and blood"—natural human resources—to comprehend. Grasping the things pertaining to Christ, however, requires our Father in heaven revealing them to us, as He did to Peter. Through the New Covenant, this ongoing revelation is offered to all believers.

THE DANCE

God has placed within us, as part of our new disposition, a new upward passion, a restless yearning to worship Him.

To the Samaritan woman, Jesus pictured this passion of the Spirit as "a fountain of water springing up into everlasting life." Elsewhere in the New Testament this word for "springing up" is translated "leaping." The tense of the word here denotes continual action. In other words, the Spirit of God within the regenerate heart of the believer is ceaselessly leaping toward heaven for communion with God and worship of the Father.

The Holy Spirit is never seen as passive in the Bible. He's always on the prowl, moving upward, moving outward. Our worship of God is to be carried out on the Spirit's coattails as He leaps incessantly toward the Father.

When we don't *feel* like this—when we think, *Forget the water springing up, just a trickle would be great*—the starting point for moving back toward God is to focus on the ceaseless exuberance of the Spirit within us. When what seems most real in our pursuit of God is apathy or dryness, has the Spirit lessened His leaping at all? No, a thousand times no. His passion for God never rides on our coattails. He keeps dancing whether or not we're at His side.

Normally (though not always), when our passion for God seems drained, it's because we've picked another partner to dance with. The Bible calls it idolatry; it's the sure drainpipe of godly passion.

The Spirit eagerly awaits us to rejoin Him in the dance. That's why repentance isn't working up a new desire or commitment to do right; it's turning a cold shoulder to those whom we've allowed to seduce us away from our original Partner and then rejoining Him in the dance of the ages. It's in His arms, with Him in the lead, that we can once again be swept up in divinely orchestrated communion and worship.

Losing Control

God never calls us to live in neutral, to exist in a vacuum. He tells us, as we saw earlier, to "be filled with the Spirit" in a manner similar to drunkenness—to be God-intoxicated saints. In essence He says, "Lose control of yourself to the domination of the Holy Spirit." What will this look like?

We find the answer in the verses immediately following the one about drunkenness and Spirit-filling. We're to be "speaking to one another in psalms and hymns and spiritual songs, singing and making melody in your heart to the Lord, giving thanks always for all things to God the Father in the name of our Lord Jesus Christ."

This upward display of affection, gratitude, and worship is the inevitable by-product of being a Spirit-dominated individual and community. We lift our voices on high not to bring heaven down to our souls, but because heaven has already been brought down to them!

Worship isn't letting music fill our hollow hearts; it's above all else an arena where God-soaked, full-hearted saints lift their voices of overwhelming thanks to Him for all He is and has done. Worship isn't something we do *for* God, but *with* God. This is why the writer of Hebrews exhorts, "Therefore *by Him* let us continually offer the sacrifice of praise." *It requires God to worship God,* and the sooner we learn this humbling reality the sooner our lives and lips will reflect the design for which they were created.

A SHOUT TO GOD—AND FROM GOD

Our love for our Father isn't a timid, restrained affair, but a Spirit-invigorated shout of filial affection. Paul says that by "the Spirit of adoption" whom we've received, "we cry out, 'Abba, Father.'" The word translated "cry out" is a strong one, carrying the image of shouting in most New Testament uses.

Where does this intensity of love come from? From God alone.

Our prayers to God, and the passion of those prayers, are from

God as well: "We do not know what we should pray for as we ought, but the Spirit Himself makes intercession for us with groanings which cannot be uttered." The sometimes inexpressible intensity and fervor of our petitions is God-originated and God-empowered. Prayer that isn't Spirit-induced is no different than what millions of pagans offer each day. But God has given His Spirit to His children so their prayers may be scented with His presence, rising up as incense before Him.

CHRISTIAN MYSTICISM

There's an undeniable mysticism to true Christian spirituality. The Spirit of God urges us upward to know and worship God the Father and God the Son, penetrating our inner being to spotlight and inflame spiritual realities.

This "Christian mysticism," Francis Schaeffer writes,

> is communion with Christ. It is Christ bringing forth fruit through me, the Christian.... There is to be experiential reality, moment by moment. And the glory of the experiential reality of the Christian, as opposed to the bare existential experience, or the religious experiences of the East, is that we can do it with all the intellectual doors and windows open. We do not need a dark room; we do not need to be under the influence of hallucinatory drugs; we do not need to be listening to a certain kind of music; we can know the reality of the supernatural here and now.

Without the Holy Spirit's illumination of these realities, we're like visitors in a darkened art museum. The portraits are just the same as when the lights were on; they didn't change by being plunged into darkness. But what a difference it makes to the beholder! He can know that great beauty lies directly in front of him, but he cannot view and admire that beauty—until the lights come back on.

When they do—when the Holy Spirit enlightens—we can begin to understand this prayer of Augustine:

You flashed, You shone;
> and You chased away my blindness.

You became fragrant;
> and I inhaled and sighed for You.

I tasted,
> and now hunger and thirst for You.

You touched me;
> and I burned for Your embrace.

POWER'S REALITY

Let me ask two searching questions that I also ask myself:

The first: If God were to withdraw His Spirit from this earth, how significantly would my spiritual life be altered? Would it come to a screeching halt, or continue on virtually unaffected?

The second: What spiritual reality is there in my life that could not be duplicated by an unbeliever, no matter how hard they tried? What blatantly supernatural evidences of God leak through me?

The same God who parted the Red Sea and raised His Son from the grave inhabits you and me. Our lives are designed to be a repeat performance of what happened at the Red Sea and at Christ's tomb. The miracles in our lives will be no less miraculous and no less dependent upon God's power for implementation. *The Christian life properly lived is an ongoing miracle*—a miracle empowered through truly knowing God.

Think deeply about all this as you read and meditate on John 17, observing the intimacy between Jesus Christ and His Father.

CHAPTER 14

A Fresh Look at Freedom in Christ

A Christian is a perfectly free lord of all, subject to none. A Christian is a perfectly dutiful servant of all, subject to all.

MARTIN LUTHER

"The word *Christian*," writes Eugene Peterson,

means different things to different people. To one person it means a stiff, uptight, inflexible way of life, colorless and unbending. To another it means a risky, surprise-filled venture, lived tiptoe at the edge of expectation.

Either of these pictures can be supported with evidence.... But if we restrict ourselves to biblical evidence, only the second image can be supported: the image of the person living zestfully, exploring every experience—pain and joy, enigma and insight, fulfillment and frustration—as a dimension of human freedom, searching through each for sense and grace. If we get our information from the biblical material, there is no doubt that the Christian life is a dancing, leaping, daring life.

Peterson speaks right to the heart of this chapter's topic. As believers we're called to stand fast in the freedom by which Christ has made us free. Ours is to be "a dancing, leaping, daring life." But too many of us are stuck in the religious mire of what has been termed "joyless moralism," holding tenaciously to moral duties but remaining disconnected from the explosive joy and freedom of the indwelling life of Christ.

One of God's intended results of the New Covenant is a Spirit-dependent lifestyle of liberty. Anything less is slavery, either to the tyranny of law-based obedience or to the bondage of flesh-driven sensuality.

"If the Son makes you free," Jesus promised, *you shall be free indeed.*" May God grant us grace and courage to leave behind the fetters of legalism or license and to soar as the golden eagles He has made us, swept along in the currents of His Spirit to the glorious adventure of supernatural living, attaining a joy that the shallow, earthly imitation called "happiness" can never touch.

Only then will we be "free indeed."

AVOIDING EXTREMES

What exactly is this thing called freedom, and how do we find and maintain it?

Whatever genuine Christian freedom is, it absolutely requires the presence and power of God's Spirit. "Where the Spirit of the Lord is, *there* is liberty," Paul says. The Spirit's presence will keep us alert to two opposing extremes that we want to avoid at all costs.

The first is to be so concerned with the potential abuse of freedom that we pull in the reins and lose the legitimate and godly exuberance that is our birthright as God's children.

Many preachers and teachers are more concerned with keeping their people morally in check than with freeing them for God's adventure of supernatural living. Yes, it's always wrong when freedom is abused, but freedom transforms and elevates a believer's walk with God to heights that stale rule-keeping never can.

Reinhold Niebuhr has well said,

> You may be able to compel people to maintain certain minimum standards by stressing duty, but the highest moral and spiritual achievements depend not upon a push but a pull. People must be charmed into righteousness.

This is why Paul writes with white-hot ink, "Stand fast therefore in the liberty by which Christ has made us free, and do not be entangled again with a yoke of bondage."

The opposite extreme is using freedom as a ticket to fleshly indulgence. Paul also warns, "Do not use liberty as an opportunity for the flesh." Such misconstrued freedom results when preachers and teachers drain away God's holiness from His love. Our flesh can quickly translate freedom in Christ into license for self-centered and sin-justifying living. This is not true freedom, but only spiritualized and rationalized bondage.

PURPOSE-DRIVEN UNRESTRAINT

I like to define true freedom in Christ as *purpose-driven unrestraint.* It's a liberty that's possible only because, in the New Covenant, we have both the desire and the power to do God's will. We're free in the fullest sense only when those two things come together. Power without desire results in begrudging obedience at best. Desire without power results in frustrated intentions. When we have both power and desire, we have the freedom of being able to do what we most deeply want to do.

One popular Bible teacher has defined freedom as "not the right to do what we want, but the ability to do what we ought." Do you see the problem with this definition? It's only half the story. It assumes that our "wants" and God's "oughts" are always opposed to each other. The wondrous beauty of the New Covenant is that God has made the "oughts" of His Word the "wants" of our regenerate heart, then flooded our inner beings with resurrection power so we can bring these to fruition. This is freedom indeed.

Then we can gladly "give in" to our divine design and say yes to God's goal for us, which is to glorify Him through Jesus Christ— "to be prisms refracting the light of God's glory into all of life," as John Piper says.

Freedom is not the ability to do that anything we want, whenever we want. Rather freedom is the ability to live responsibly the truth

EXHILARATION of our relationship with God and with one another – Pope John Paul II

We do well to remember that the word *freedom* meant much more to the original readers of the New Testament than it does to us. Over half the population in the Roman world was enslaved. Aristotle's view was widely held: "A slave is a living tool, just as a tool is an inanimate slave."

To experience freedom, therefore, went beyond being unbound; it meant exhilaration—the dancing and leaping that Peterson spoke of.

Freedom in Christ is a spiritually intoxicating wine, a breathtaking flight into space, a soul-thrilling escape from enemy territory. It's the spiritual exhilaration of having one's soul set free for the high adventure of a God-enabled assault upon life.

THE RIGHT MASTER

Paradoxically, ultimate freedom also means being enslaved to the right master. Virtually every passage in the New Testament dealing with freedom contains immediate references to slavery as well. This shouldn't surprise us. In reality there's no such thing as absolute freedom; the only real freedom man has is the freedom to choose his master.

We're all enslaved, either to God or to sin and idols. We all go through life as driven people; the only question is who we've chosen to put in the driver's seat. We may be comfort-driven, approval-driven, security-driven, achievement-driven, wealth-driven, fitness-driven, health-driven, ministry-driven, or Christ-driven. Never, ever, are *we* alone in control.

"Having been *set free* from sin," Paul tells believers, "you *became slaves* of righteousness." As Christians, our experience of freedom continues only while we choose to stay within our new bondage to righteousness. There's no such thing as joint citizenship between righteousness and sin. We're no longer free to fully enjoy frolicking in sin, because the yearning for righteousness that's now deep within us always tags along to the party.

Being "free indeed," Jesus said, comes only when "*the Son* makes you free." True freedom comes only by yielding to His authority, His presence, and His power. As we radically abandon ourselves to our rightful Master, we'll find ourselves in glad bondage, and our souls will sing for joy at coming home. We'll find that the tension is gone between the standard of God's demands and our inner reluctance and inability to meet them. That which was imposed upon us externally is now implanted within us supernaturally through His New Covenant provision of our new disposition and power.

I've found again and again in my own life how this truth helps me know if I'm operating out of the flesh or the Spirit. There's always an inner tenseness when I'm trying to do the will of God out of my flesh. It's a heaviness within, a kind of grasping that never feels clean. When the Spirit is in control, there's an inner relaxation, a sense of something flowing that I'm not having to work at, a joyous boldness that feels dependently clean.

FORWARD IN FREEDOM

Freedom always involves two things—what we've been set free *from* and what we've been set free *for*.

What is it that we need freedom *from*?

The answer from Jesus is *sin:* "Most assuredly, I say to you, whoever commits sin is a slave of sin." And now, because of the New Covenant, we can say with Paul, "The law of the Spirit of life in Christ Jesus has made me free from the law of sin and death."

Religion never helped anyone get out of sin; it only ruins their perception of sin's presence in their life. Christ alone can pull us out of sin's quicksand. Only He can make "free indeed" saints.

But biblical freedom is never spiritual anarchy or a new ability to enjoy forbidden things. We're released *from* bondage to sin and death and the law, and we're liberated *for* obedience in the Spirit— *from* a lower bondage, *for* a higher one.

That's why freedom in Christ leads directly in Scripture to truly loving others. Paul says, "Do not use liberty as an opportunity for the flesh, but *through love serve one another*. For all the law is fulfilled in one word, even in this: 'You shall *love your neighbor as yourself.*'"

We're a community of free men and women—free from grim,

duty-driven spirituality…free from the tyranny of needing others' approval…free from the darkness of guilt that blankets our souls…free from the quicksand of sin's power. Let the trumpets blow, the cymbals sound, the dance begin. God calls us to savor fully every drop of our Christ-begotten liberty. But He also has another agenda for this exhilaration of spirit. It's to move us spontaneously outward to dispense His love into the lives of others. Remember that outside the dance hall of our newfound freedom is a world of broken, hurting people, desperately in need of what we're enjoying. Compelled by gifted compassion, we're called to a lifestyle of serving them in love as bondservants of God.

MATURE FREEDOM

Our freedom to truly love highlights what I like to call the difference between adolescent freedom and mature freedom.

Adolescent freedom asks only, What am I free *from?* Mature freedom asks also, What am I free *for?*

Adolescent freedom asks only, Is it forbidden? Mature freedom asks also, Is it helpful?

Adolescent freedom embraces the liberty "to do my own thing"; mature freedom embraces the liberty "to do Christ's thing."

Adolescent freedom often confuses legalism with obedience; mature freedom understands the difference.

Mature freedom knows not only the exhilaration of being free from the wrong master, but also the greater exhilaration of being enslaved to the right Master.

Mature freedom recognizes that one is both free and a servant to others, as Luther noted: A Christian is both "a perfectly free lord of all" and "a perfectly dutiful servant of all."

Mature freedom realizes not only freedom from others' opinions, but also concern for the "weak." Mature freedom enjoys liberty but feels no need to prove it.

OBSTACLES TO TRUE FREEDOM

What keeps us from fully living out the exhilaration of New Covenant liberty? And what happens if we revert back to Old Covenant bondage?

In Paul's day, the Christians of Galatia had begun well as New Covenant saints by living through Christ, but all too soon they reverted to an Old Covenant approach of living under a code. They had allowed themselves to be seduced away from depending on Christ alone for their spirituality and added legalism. But adding to Christ always short-circuits our experience of His fullness and stifles our freedom. In the book of Galatians we see how their joy evaporated, their love retreated, their souls became agitated, pressure overwhelmed them, guilt blanketed them, and their focus became distorted. The Galatians failed to understand that as we're absorbed with and dependent upon the *Son* of God, the *standards* of God take care of themselves.

As much as anything else, what I like to call "living by a list" is where New Covenant freedom is lost. Many of us begin our day by making a mental or written list of things that need to be done for the day to be spent profitably. There's nothing wrong with that. A list can be a wonderful tool for helping organize and prioritize what we sense God has called us to. The problem comes when the list becomes a master instead of a tool. Freedom is never lost by a list; it's lost through *living* by the list.

We let our activities and interactions during the day be driven by the "god" of list completion. Our sense of success rests squarely in the hands of getting as many items checked off as possible. People are viewed as interruptions (unless they happen to be an item on our list). Our prayers through the day (if there are any) will primarily be calls to enlist God's aid for doing what we need to get our list completed.

And when our day is over, when we put our head on the pillow, we'll feel one of two things.

Most days we'll feel at least mildly discouraged and very tired, since most of us make lists for ourselves that no mortal can keep. (I'm no exception.)

Or, on those few days when we accomplish our list, we'll lay down with a quiet smugness. *Lord, I thank you that I am not like other people who cannot keep their lists.* We'll experience the false security of discharged duties. Never mind that my wife never felt cared about, that I brushed by my children, that those in the office felt no warmth from me whatsoever, and everybody noticed my agitation whenever my schedule was interrupted. *I checked off my list,* and under an Old Covenant approach to life, that's what matters.

What would this same day look like if we lived from a New Covenant approach?

It's very possible that our list itself might look exactly the same. The list itself is neutral, and New Covenant living is no refuge from responsible, purposeful living. But at the least, the list would be *prayed over.* Our primary question underlying the list would not be, "What do I need to get done today?" but "Lord, what do You desire to do through me today?"

As we went about the day, we would work diligently to fulfill the tasks before us, but this would not be our primary goal. Our highest goal would be to abide in the Vine and let His life spill forth unhindered, so He could walk through us, work through us, speak through us, and most of all love through us.

We would view the people we encountered not as interruptions but as opportunities to fulfill our high calling to love others with God's love. We would in fact recognize that God had the right to "interrupt" our list at any time.

And when we lay our head down at night, our New Covenant day would leave us sensing two things.

First, humble gratitude. We would keenly realize that anything and everything worthwhile we had done that day had been done *through* us, not *by* us.

Second, we would sense a measure of joy—joy for what God had accomplished through us, and joy that anything not accomplished that day because of our own disobedience had been washed clean by the blood of the Lamb. We might also feel convicted by the Holy Spirit of moments when we blocked and checked God in our lives, but having honestly confessed these, we could go to sleep worshiping a God who keeps no list of our transgressions.

How do *you* feel at the end of a typical day? Are you still somehow in bondage to a list, whether mental or written?

Look back at this chapter's comparison of adolescent freedom with mature freedom. In what ways are the perspectives of mature freedom not yet fully yours? In particular, how free are you to fully love those whom God has placed in your life?

To spur your thoughts, meditate on Galatians 5 and 6 and study in 1 Corinthians 9 how the apostle Paul used his freedom, as you compare his convictions and commitments with your own.

CHAPTER 15

A Fresh Look at Community

It is our care for the helpless, our practice of loving-kindness, that brands us in the eyes of many of our opponents. "Look!" they say, "How they love one another! Look how they are prepared to die for one another."

TERTULLIAN

People who were there still talk about it. It happened years ago at the Seattle Special Olympics, a competition for physically and mentally disabled children. The hundred-yard dash had nine entrants. The gun sounded and the runners started out as fast as they were able. Then one little boy tripped, fell on the track, and began to sob. The other eight heard his cry and all stopped to turn and look. Seeing him on the ground, they walked back to him—every one of them.

One little girl with Down syndrome bent down, kissed his leg, and said, "This will make it better." Then all nine put their arms around one another and walked together to the finish line. Everyone in the stadium stood and applauded, their cheers continuing for several minutes.

Even as I write this I find it hard to hold back tears. What is it about this true story that touches something deep within me and brought a stadium full of people to their feet?

Maybe it awakens our intuitive sense that there's something of greater importance in life than individual success. It reminds us that we were created to be interdependent, and that life was never intended to be lived solo, but in tandem. As human beings created in the image of God, we crave the oneness that the triune God enjoys incessantly—Father, Son, Holy Spirit in perfect unity, dynamic community, satisfying intimacy. (It must be a blast to be God!) Perhaps the image of those nine handicapped children walking arm-in-arm toward the finish line touches that divine imprint within us, causing it to rise up and whisper, *There! That's how you were designed to live!*

Maybe it also reminds us that we're all handicapped travelers on this treacherous planet…needing desperately to stay in lockstep as we sojourn together.

RESTORING OUR CONNECTIONS

Francis Schaeffer points out that at the Fall, mankind disconnected not only from God, but also from ourselves and from others. The oneness that had flowed naturally and effortlessly between Adam and Eve was now shattered.

And yet we cannot shake free of our image-bearer yearning for relationship with others. We must either divert it or deny it.

In his famous song decades ago about being a rock and an island, Paul Simon included lines about hiding in his room with his books to protect him. I find myself relating to those lyrics more than I wish; my flesh, left to itself, would go in exactly that direction.

For years, even after I became a believer, if you gave me the choice between hiding in a book or interacting with a person, the book would win out every time. I still have a long way to go in this, but I can honestly say there are many times now I'd choose a person over a book (not that this is *always* the right choice). I can also say with every fiber of my being that this change has come only through the supernatural work of God's grace in my heart. It helps confirm to me that these New Covenant realities are not only true, but have life-changing power.

Like all the connections we lost at the Fall, God-honoring unity and deeply satisfying community can begin to be restored only through our New Covenant provisions.

Not an Ideal, but Reality

In the New Covenant, God made this promise for His people: "I will give them one heart." The only solution for our inbred disconnectedness with one another is God's determined resolve—*I will*—and His grace—I will *give*. God and God alone is the foundation and source for our new community.

Our true unity is God-originated, Christ-purchased, Spirit-sustained. Our truest bond is never based on our group or cause, our denomination or theological camp, the spiritual experiences we have in common, or the kind of ministry we're involved in—but always on our common Christ. He is the foundation of our common fellowship, made possible by a common death. We are indwelt by a common Spirit and designed for a common purpose.

This is why, as Dietrich Bonhoeffer wrote, "Christian brotherhood is not an ideal which we must realize; it is rather a reality created by God in Christ in which we may participate." Unity is not something to be achieved, but to be kept intact. Paul tells us "to *keep* [not "achieve" or "produce"] the unity of the Spirit in the bond of peace." You can "keep" only what was already present.

And this harmony is "of the Spirit"; it's God-produced, not man-manufactured.

So often we approach unity from a fundamentally Old Covenant approach, frantically trying to make it happen and produce something we believe is fundamentally absent. But the unshakable reality is that *whenever* two believers meet, unity *is* present; the only question is whether it's being actualized.

LOVE OR MANIPULATION?

That actualization is called *love*.

It's *agape* love, an others-centeredness that is so radical it can *only* be produced by God.

Paul prays, "May the Lord make you *increase and abound in love* to one another," words that might better be translated, "*fill up* and *overflow* in love." Our lives are to be riverbeds, spilling over with love into other people's lives.

This love is from the storehouse of heaven and comes to us only through the Holy Spirit. We're to enjoy this love as deeply as possible, then distribute it as potently and widely as possible.

We are distributors, not manufacturers, and our primary commodity to distribute among men is a love they've never seen in the unsaved world.

But we must be overwhelmed by it ourselves before we'll be able to dispense this love effectively. Therefore Paul prays that we'll first be "filled up" and *then* "overflowing." We can't give away what we don't have. When our souls feel inwardly destitute, loving others will seem like an expensive project for which we have insufficient funds. Most likely we'll find a way to back off. If our responsibility to love seems to significantly outweigh our resources, a kind of internal implosion causes us to pull back from getting involved.

At the same time, our own empty hearts and parched souls cry out for relief. Before long, we'll view others as watering holes for quenching our thirst; their affection and approval will no longer be something we *enjoy,* but something we *require.* We'll give them right of entry into the place in our heart's temple that belongs only to God. When this happens, they've stopped being people and become idols.

Our approach to others shifts subtly from ministry to manipulation, as Larry Crabb describes it. Ministry is giving with nothing required in return. Manipulation is also giving, but always with a hook attached. It is get-driven giving, and others sense it in us intuitively and back off. As they fail to meet our expectations, the result is that our anger and frustration escalate.

Genuine community can never take place where believers fail to appropriate and operate from supernatural resources. God has designed His new community so that its success requires Him. When His resources are neglected, the dryness in our hearts and the poverty of our own fleshly resources will cause relating with one another to degenerate into varying degrees of people-draining.

This doesn't mean it's wrong to enjoy or benefit from another believer's part in our life. Nor does it mean we should deny our real need of each other and think that our individual relationship with God is all that's really necessary for spirituality. Bonhoeffer saw the balance: "Let him who cannot be alone beware of community. Let him who is not in community beware of being alone."

To Each Other's Fields

The reality is that every believer is rich beyond measure when it comes to God's provisions for significant community. We're blessed "with every spiritual blessing in the heavenly places in Christ," and at the top of that blessing list is the kind of love that flows ceaselessly among the Trinity.

A Jewish fable tells the story of two brothers, both farmers, who lived next to each other. After a particularly bountiful harvest, each brother had to decide what to do with his surplus.

The first brother said to himself, "Here I am with a wife and children, but my lonely brother has no one. I think I'll surprise him by taking some of my crop and placing it in his field."

The other brother thought, "Here I am single. My brother has a wife and children to care for, and I don't need anywhere near what I have. I think I'll surprise him and put some of my crop in his field."

So the brothers caught each other at midnight, stealing into the other's field to leave their blessing.

New Covenant community is moving forward into one another's fields to give from the supernatural bounty we've received out of the overwhelming supply of the Spirit.

The Difference It Makes

Why is God so keenly interested that His children be well connected and dynamically united?

The answer we usually think of first is that our unity will help strengthen and encourage one another toward greater godliness. We view community primarily as a laboratory for our Christian development.

But God primarily sees our community as an exhibition, not a laboratory. Our Spirit-drenched oneness is the most important way His spectacularness is displayed on earth.

In the first centuries of the church, the supernatural concern and oneness among believers rocked the world back on its heels. "It is incredible to see the fervor with which the people of that religion help each other in their wants," wrote the second-century writer Lucian. "Their first legislator [Jesus] has put it into their heads that they are brethren."

In our relationships with each other, there's more at stake than simply enjoying one another's company, wonderful as that can be. God has designed for public display a network of diverse individuals whose lives are so beautifully interconnected that it's nothing short of stunning. The name of this network is the *church,* God's "called out ones." Our specialty is to be a relational excellence that unmistakably reflects the love within and between the Trinity.

In Paul's prayer for the Roman Christians, look at the purpose he saw for their unity: "Now may the God of patience and comfort grant you to be like-minded toward one another, according to Christ Jesus, that you may with one mind and one mouth glorify the God and Father of our Lord Jesus Christ."

Paul then added this instruction: "Therefore *receive* [this can be translated, "warmly welcome"] *one another,* just as Christ also received us, *to the glory of God.*" The main reason we're to warmly welcome one another in Christlike fashion isn't what it does for the other person or for us, but what it does for God. Never does the world see Christ more clearly than when His love flows freely among believers.

The same purpose was in the heart of Jesus as He prayed for you and me and our brothers and sisters: "that they may all be one, as You, Father, are in Me, and I in You; that they also may be one in Us, *that the world may believe that You sent Me.*" Our unity, Francis Schaeffer says, is our "final apologetic." By this, more than anything else, non-Christians will pass judgment on whether or not Christianity is true.

The vast majority of people who I've seen trust Christ over the years didn't do so through a one-shot message or gospel presentation. Most of them began their pilgrimage toward Christ by hanging around the fringes of a group of believers. They became intrigued with how these believers cared for one another. Their curiosity was aroused; they had never seen anything like it. Their eventual coming to Christ is a direct answer to Christ's high priestly prayer two thousand years ago.

When it's all said and done, the song is right—they'll know we are Christians by our love.

Group Project

As the highest purpose for our community, God's glory embraces many other purposes as well. For our sakes as well as His own, God has given us other members of the body to benefit from, not quarrel with or disdain.

C. S. Lewis recalled that when he first became a Christian,

> I thought I could do it on my own, by retiring to my rooms and reading theology, and I wouldn't go to the churches and gospel halls. I disliked very much their hymns, which I considered to be fifth-rate poems set to sixth-rate music. But as I went on I saw the great merit of it. I came up against differ-

ent people of quite different outlooks and different education, and then gradually my conceit just began peeling off.

I realized that the hymns (which were just sixth-rate
music) were, nevertheless, being sung with devotion and
benefit by an old saint in elastic-side boots in the opposite
pew, and then you realize that you aren't fit to clean those
boots. It gets you out of your solitary conceit.

Our Christian growth is a group project rather than an occasion for "solitary conceit." Community is the soil in which believers most readily mature.

Together we're commanded to "consider one another in order
to stir up love and good works, not forsaking the assembling of
ourselves together, as is the manner of some, but exhorting one
another." The word used in this passage for "stir up" means "to
incite, stimulate, create a fever." Our community is to generate an
internal heat that excites each one of us toward God-honoring living.

God gives us other believers also to lovingly point out when
we're being deceived by sin, something true friends in Christ are
willing to do.

True fellowship differs from mere human friendship in the role
that the supernatural plays. True fellowship moves believers closer
to God as well as to one another. Do you know someone in whose
presence you often feel your heart for God kindled? When was the
last time you finished a conversation with another believer and left
thinking, "I want to know Christ more deeply," or "I want to step
out and risk what I know God is calling me to"? I can think now of
a few men who do this consistently for me, and their friendship is
one of the great treasures of my life.

When David was in trouble, Jonathan went to him and "strengthened his hand in God." In this way he encouraged David to take the risk of staying his course. Do you have someone who "strengthens your hand in God"? Someone who not only comforts and encourages, but urges you, through God, to cut loose from the moorings of living safely in the harbor and to move out into the risky but joyous waters of what Christ is calling you to? Are you that kind of person for someone else?

ALL LOWLINESS AND MEEKNESS

In Paul's letter to the Ephesians, God commands us to "walk worthy of the calling with which you were called"—in other words, let your behavior on earth worthily display your inheritance in Christ. Live like the billionaire you are!

As Paul goes on in this passage to describe the practical outworking of our resources in Christ, he focuses first on community—as if to say that the most important place our newfound wealth is to be displayed is in how we relate to one another. Paul points to the essential attitudes we need in order to keep intact the reality of our God-given unity—"all lowliness and gentleness" (with this second word better translated as "meekness"). Do our lives evidence this brokenness of spirit and a humble yielding to others?

The great eighteenth-century preachers John Wesley and George Whitefield supported each other until their emerging doctrinal differences (Arminianism versus Calvinism) caused a rift between them. They later reconciled and remained good friends, but not all their followers were so gracious.

The story is told that, after Whitefield's death, a follower of

Wesley asked him, "Do you suppose you will see Mr. Whitefield in heaven?" Wesley, detecting her assessment that Whitefield wasn't truly a believer, responded that he didn't expect to see Whitefield there.

The woman eagerly pressed him. "Then you don't really believe he was converted?"

"Converted? Of course he's converted," Wesley responded. "But I do not expect to see him in heaven because he will be so close to the throne of God, and I so far away, that I doubt I will be able to see him."

If only this same "lowliness and meekness" were more pervasive among Christians today!

Significantly, the two Greek words for "lowliness" and "gentleness" are also placed side by side in the passage where Jesus says, "I am gentle and lowly in heart." Christ calls us to display His own qualities, which He Himself has already placed within us.

Let me stress this once more: While spiritual unity is a gift, it's a gift that must be preserved and maintained. And let me suggest five critical areas in which we must be alert to preserve and maintain our oneness in Christ:

1. *An unforgiving spirit toward others.*
2. *Unwillingness to confront those who have sinned against us.*
3. *Unwillingness to reconcile with those whom we've knowingly wronged.*
4. *Receiving or passing along gossip.*
5. *Judging other believers over nonessential issues.*

Making the most of our New Covenant provisions and liberty means the freedom to major on the majors and not let nonessentials preoccupy or divide us. It means learning to distinguish between issues that are genuinely biblical and those that are matters of only personality, culture, or tradition—such as worship styles, political involvement, education choices for our children, and so on. We can relax as we recognize that equally committed believers may come to exactly the opposite conclusion about such an issue and be right at the same time, as Paul clearly demonstrates in Romans 14.

This is why one of the greatest needs in the body of Christ, and one of the most important ingredients for sustained unity, is simply *mutual respect* toward one another—on these issues as well as in all other areas. A centuries-old Christian maxim beautifully summarizes it: "In essentials unity; in non-essentials liberty; in all things charity."

As you prayerfully assess yourself in these areas, I encourage you to meditate on the unifying truths in Ephesians 4.

CHAPTER 16

A Fresh Look
at Ministry

God's deepest purpose for the world is to fill it with reverberations
of His glory in the lives of a new humanity.

JOHN PIPER

The nineteenth-century English clergyman Frederic William
Farrar pictured every believer's soul as "a cavern full of gems."

The casual observer glances into it through some cranny, and
all looks dark and sullen and useless. But let light enter into
and lo! It will flash with crystals and amethysts and quiver
under the touch of brightness.

If souls do not shine before you it is because you bring
them no light to make them shine. Throw away your miserable, smouldering, fuming torch of conceit and hatred, lift
up to them the light of love, and lo! They will arise and
shine; yea, flame and burn with an undreamt of glory.

What does it mean to minister to others in such a way as to
cause God's light to fall on their hidden gems, making them blaze
forth for His glory?

THE CONTRAST

"Our sufficiency is from God," Paul says, "who also made us sufficient as *ministers of the new covenant.*" What does it look like to
minister to others from a New Covenant approach?

This same passage is where Paul says, "The letter kills, but the
Spirit gives life." Old Covenant ministry breeds death. A ministry
that merely lays before people a code to live by—and reproves
them for not being disciplined or committed enough to keep it—
drains away vitality, joy, and hope.

But New Covenant ministry infuses life as it spotlights the
excellence of Christ and the outlandish resources He has provided
for us, as it calls us to the high adventure of living unreservedly for
the King of kings.

Paul speaks also in this passage of the Old Covenant "ministry
of condemnation." Old Covenant ministry is shame-based and
guilt-driven as it focuses primarily on where we fall short of God's
standards.

But New Covenant arouses hope—confident expectation and
blazing optimism. While it doesn't back away at all from confronting sin and disobedience, it always moves beyond the failure
to the possibility. It seeks to arouse the godly inclination in all
believers to know God more deeply, to hunger for His best, and to
move forward in His power to the only way of life that can genuinely satisfy their new hearts.

New Covenant ministry, like the New Covenant itself, is a radically new and better way to stimulate growth in believers' lives. It's
working *with* God in helping other believers fulfill their whole
potential in Christ.

What It Looks Like

Imagine chatting with a Christian friend who confides that he's feeling guilty for not praying more. He asks you for help and advice.

If you answer from an Old Covenant approach, you might say something like this:

"You know, John, God specifically commands us to pray. In fact He says to pray without ceasing. It seems to me that if praying were important enough to you, you could find the time. It doesn't matter whether you feel like it or not; what matters is whether you're going to obey Him. If you're going to be a committed believer, prayer is one of the most important disciplines you need to be practicing."

On the other hand, a New Covenant approach might be this:

"When you became a believer, John, one of the many great things that happened to you is that God placed within you a desire to communicate with Him. This desire can never be taken away, because God made the promise to give His people a heart to know Him. I know that this desire may not seem real to you right now, but I can assure you it's still there.

"In fact, my guess is that even as we're talking, you're beginning to sense this desire stirring within you. Prayer is one of the primary ways we communicate with God, and for you to experience the kind of intimacy with Him that I know you want to have, you need to unleash your desire to talk with Him. That's what prayer is really all about. And you know what? God Himself will give you strength and even wisdom for your praying.

"I know you want more out of your relationship with God than you're tasting now, and prayer offers you such a big part of experiencing God's best for your life."

The Foundation for New Covenant Ministry

I'm sure you can easily recognize by now that an absolute necessity in our New Covenant ministry is for us to be held hostage by these New Covenant realities ourselves. We must be glad discoverers and possessors of a treasure we never dreamed existed, in order to help others see and take hold of it.

New Covenant ministers must first of all be New Covenant connoisseurs. Our lives are to have the fragrance of God all over them, an aroma that only the Holy Spirit can produce.

New Covenant ministry is also based upon very positive, God-given assumptions about every believer. A New Covenant approach to ministry views all believers through *fundamentally optimistic lenses.* "From now on," Paul says, "we regard no one according to the flesh.... If anyone is in Christ, he is a new creation; old things have passed away; behold, all things have become new." Or to put it another way, we no longer view believers primarily in light of their *problems* but in light of their *potential* because of the Holy Spirit dwelling within them.

Fellow brothers and sisters in Christ are not just forgiven sinners. They are silver saints who possess something wonderful beneath the tarnish of their sinful nature. For every believer there's something deeper in them than their sin, no matter how obscured it may be.

What You Can Know for Certain

What are these positive assumptions you can be certain of for every believer?

First, every Christian you encounter is of immense value and importance. Not only did Christ die for them, but God also has uniquely designed them to be an exhibition of the supernatural—a reflection of His craftsmanship. This is true for *every* believer; there are no disposable saints. We're all "His workmanship, created in Christ Jesus for good works, which God prepared beforehand that we should walk in them." To help accomplish these divinely ordained good works, God has also given each believer one or more spiritual gifts for carrying out His will.

Therefore our calling is not to help other believers fulfill what *we* think is the will of God for their lives, but to help them hear the voice of God *for themselves* and find their unique, God-designed, God-gifted calling.

With every believer you encounter, we can also assume this person will never be fully satisfied until his or her life is fully aligned with God's uniquely designed purposes. No matter how content he may look on the outside, there'll be some measure of internal restlessness if this believer's life is out of alignment with God's purposes.

Sometimes I'll ask a Christian brother, "Do you feel like you're hitting on all six cylinders spiritually, in terms of the direction your life is headed?" Or, "If you were to die tomorrow, would you basically be satisfied with how you've spent the last few years of your life?" Very often the answer is "no," and then I can begin to help him explore the reasons.

We can also assume that every believer we encounter has divinely implanted resources that are pressing outward for release. Our calling is not to make something happen within him but simply to help release what God has already set in motion.

Jesus made this promise for every believer: "Out of his heart will flow rivers of living water." The waters of the life of Christ relentlessly push forward for expression within all of us. Some believers may not be aware of this, but they cannot thwart its reality. If the waters aren't making their way past the surface, it's not because they've stopped pressing, but because the believer has shut the floodgates of his life for one reason or another. Our responsibility is *not* to get the waters moving, but to cooperate with the Holy Spirit in helping open up those gates again.

THE MESSAGES YOU CONVEY

Christlike love is the lifeblood of our ministry, for Christ's New Covenant command is to love one another *as He loved us.* As we seek to love other believers in this way, what messages will our love convey?

The first is this: *I'm relentlessly and unconditionally for you. You can never extinguish my love for you.*

Our love is to be like the love of Christ, who loved His disciples "to the end," even as they denied and deserted Him. It's a love that "bears all things, believes all things, hopes all things, endures all things," a love that "never fails." This love communicates loudly and clearly, "You do not have to change in order to maintain my love for you."

At times it may need to be a tough love. It might even require, if absolutely necessary, breaking fellowship with the loved one, though this is always to be done out of love and never for lack of it. The key issue is that our ministry be bathed in a supernatural, relentless love for the ones God has privileged us to influence.

Dave Anderson (who later became my brother-in-law) was the first man to disciple me; he was the individual God used more than any other to lay the foundation for my spiritual walk and ministry.

When I met Dave, I was just beginning to grow as a Christian. I had no idea how wise and knowledgeable he was concerning the Word of God. And frankly, I didn't care. What I do remember, and what God used to draw me to him, was the fact that he was one of the first men who I sensed deeply cared for me. Dave was the first man I remember hugging me. He always seemed to have time for me. It was this unconditional, relentless love that God used to open me up to wanting to learn more about how to walk with God. His seminary degree meant nothing to me, but His Christ-bathed concern was irresistible.

Another message our love should communicate is this: *I see your potential for the kingdom of God and it excites me. I'll do all I can to help see this purpose realized.*

New Covenant love is as purposeful as it is unconditional. I like to think of it this way: True love provides both a *home* and a *business*. It provides a home in the sense that the loved one enjoys the safe place of love's unfailing warmth. It provides a business in the sense that the loved one is encouraged to find and live out his calling, thereby fulfilling what he was made for.

A final message our love should send is this: *I'll do all I can to help inflame your new nature. I'll also stand against your flesh when necessary.*

Again, both aspects are critical. True love requires that we be wise physicians, knowing when to nourish the healthy tissue and when to do battle against the cancer.

GOD: PRESENT OR ABSENT?

New Covenant ministry is, above all else, working with God—not working *for* God, but *with* Him. The distinction between these two is literally the difference between the presence or absence of God in our ministry.

He hasn't delegated something as serious as *His* ministry into unaided hands like yours or mine. What He has set out for us to do, He fully intends to do *Himself.*

Yet He has chosen to do this through the unlikely medium of flesh and blood, you and me. As in Zechariah's day, our ministry from beginning to end is to be shot through with our Lord's key ingredient for success: "'Not by might nor by power, but by My Spirit,' says the LORD of hosts."

We see this modeled most astonishingly in the life of our Lord. Listen closely to His words:

"Most assuredly, I say to you, the Son can do nothing of Himself, but what He sees the Father do; for whatever He does, the Son also does in like manner."

"My Father has been working until now, and I have been working."

"I can of Myself do nothing.… I do not seek My own will but the will of the Father who sent Me."

"The Father who dwells in Me does the works."

Jesus did nothing of His own initiative but joined in with what God was already doing. God the Father was always in the lead.

Jesus did nothing of His own invention. He was dependent upon His Father's example and sought only to mirror what He saw His Father doing.

Jesus did nothing of His own will. He didn't come to establish and fulfill His own ministry but the one designated for Him by the Father.

Jesus did nothing in His own strength. The ministry He unleashed upon the world was done wholly through the power of His indwelling Father.

In true New Covenant ministry, each of these will be true about us as well. "As the Father has sent Me," Jesus said, "I also send you." Our ministry is as tied to Christ as Christ's was to His Father!

Following Your Leader

In the Old Testament, the children of Israel were led through the wilderness by God's presence in a pillar of cloud and a pillar of fire. They had to be ready to move out or stop whenever the Lord commanded. It was never their prerogative to launch out and afterward seek God's blessings on their efforts. They were merely to keep in step with where God sovereignly decided to take them. The blessing of God's presence wasn't so much something to pray for as keep up with.

So it is with us.

New Covenant ministers wait to hear the voice of God and follow the Spirit's lead as He takes them to their individual battle stations.

This requires being still enough before God so that the static of our lives doesn't muffle His voice. It means waiting to hear His voice. It requires being humbly responsive to what He says so that we're ready to move when He moves.

How do we hear that voice and know His leading? We'll hear it in the Scriptures first and foremost, combined with prayer. It may also be through the Spirit's internal prompting, through the desire of your regenerate heart, through a sense of internal peace, through the counsel of godly friends, or through circumstances. Each of these means can be abused or misunderstood, and those that are more subjective must always be weighed in the light of Scripture.

Nonetheless, we can be assured that God is a personal, communicative Father who delights to lead His children. "He calls his own sheep by name and leads them out.... He goes before them; and the sheep follow him, for they know his voice." We must take care not to quench His working in this regard.

While the goal of New Covenant ministry is working with God to help others fulfill their whole potential in Christ, the means of doing this involves three central issues.

Nourishing the New Nature

We can nourish and inflame the new nature in other believers by words and actions that highlight their new purity, affirm their new identity, arouse their new disposition, and remind them of their new power.

One young man told me of how profoundly a Christian coach in high school had influenced him. As a student, David (not his real name) was sometimes tempted to spread his wings and launch out in directions he knew he shouldn't go. The coach would walk up behind him and say, for his ears only, "David, you're better than that," then walk off. No lecture, no discussion. David said this was all it took to get him turned back around. Why was it so powerful? Because the coach powerfully affirmed David's new identity.

Expressions like the following, at appropriate times, can help believers focus on New Covenant realities:

"That was out of character for you."

"That's not the real you I know."

"This is where your flesh is showing."

"What do you *really* want?"

"Did that feel clean to you?"

"What do you enjoy doing in ministry?"

"I know you have a good heart and that you want..."

Each of those phrases helps either to affirm their new identity or arouse their new disposition.

A reminder of their new power might look something like this: "I'm excited to see what God will do through you." It's pointless, and actually dishonest, to tell believers, "*You* can do it." We *can't* do it! It takes the Holy Spirit for any good to come forth from our lives. How blessed are those who have friends to remind them of this.

EXPOSING SIN

New Covenant ministry is anything but soft on sin. In fact, the New Covenant heightens the grievousness of sin, because God has now done *everything*—short of taking away our free wills—to make righteous living both desirable and possible.

Therefore sin is never a mistake, a weakness, a slip-up. It's moral rebellion against an unspeakably good and holy God as well as a perverse deviation from our true personhood. And it must be faced as such.

In confronting the Corinthians, Paul exposed the awfulness of their sin in no uncertain terms, as in this passage:

Do you not know that your bodies are members of Christ?
Shall I then take the members of Christ and make them
members of a harlot? Certainly not! Or do you not know
that he who is joined to a harlot is one body with her? For
"the two," He says, "shall become one flesh."

In essence Paul is saying, "Don't think you can check Jesus along with your cloak at the door as you go in to visit the local prostitute, then pick Him back up on your way out and go your way as though nothing has happened. No, a thousand times, no! When you're with a prostitute, you still have Jesus with you, like it or not. In fact, you force Him to become one flesh with her. Can you think of anything more morally despicable?"

One of the most important means for helping believers under-stand the gravity of their sin is to illustrate it for them, as Nathan did for David after his sin involving Bathsheba. I remember coun-seling once with a man who was verbally abusing his children almost daily, but he couldn't see that what he was doing was all that wrong. I posed this scenario to him:

"Suppose you knew a man who, when he came home from work each evening, would take his children into the backyard, line them up, and throw a rock or two at each one. Bruised and bloody, the children would then go inside and get on with the rest of their evening. What would you think about that man's actions?"

The father responded that he would be outraged, but he didn't really see the point of the story until I said he was doing exactly that to his own children. His words were like rocks, deeply pene-trating and wounding their souls. "I know that this is the last thing you want, deep down, to be doing to your kids," I told him. The image helped him begin to face the vileness of his actions.

As we noted earlier, because of the New Covenant, sin is not only vile, it's lunacy. In fact, I've also become increasingly con-vinced that until believers see that their sin is as *foolish* as it is *wrong*, they aren't likely to change. This is why I like to compare sin to chocolate-covered Alpo. So often we forget that the pleasure of sin really is passing, and all that is left is a mushy, grimy, joy-depleted aftertaste.

A Bare Plot, or a Garden?

A third key focal point for New Covenant ministry is strongly beckoning believers to a more God-honoring and personally satisfying plane of living.

The reality, as we saw earlier, is that the two are actually one in the same. Because of the New Covenant, saints are most deeply satisfied in the interior of their beings when God is most fully glorified in the totality of their lives.

New Covenant spirituality calls us to far more than *moralism*—which is simply the absence of that which is wrong. The New Covenant beckons us to *godliness,* the unmistakable presence of supernatural good. Morality by itself is a bare plot of land where the weeds have been pulled; godliness is a weedless garden filled with the flowers of heaven in full bloom.

Godliness always walks the second mile beyond where mere moralism stops. After commanding that the thief "steal no longer," Paul adds, "Rather let him labor, working with his hands what is good, that he may have something to give to him who has need." The same hands that once took *from* others' pockets are now to work honorably to put money *into* the pockets of those in need.

In all facets of New Covenant ministry, we must be sure we're inviting believers to nothing short of a lifestyle that *requires* God. This life is utterly Spirit-dependent from beginning to end, and anything less is a quenching of the Spirit, no matter how morally respectable it may appear.

The bottom line behind all New Covenant application is this—what it does in making God more patently visible on the playing field of life.

As you consider both your life and your ministry, I encourage you to ponder and apply the truths and examples you find in 2 Corinthians 4, 5, and 6.

Time for a Revolution

My fervent hope is that what you have discovered in this book will lead you to more and more of the glorious adventure of supernatural living, causing you by God's grace to soar to new heights of Spirit-wrought godliness and impact.

This soaring will inevitably take us into the dark and turbulent winds of suffering, trials, and heartache. While this hasn't been an issue I've addressed throughout this book, it's a large and critical part of godly living. The Scriptures promise us undeserved suffering and admonish us to endure it as part of our calling. However, we're called not just to suffer, but to suffer *well*—in a God-honoring fashion that displays the supernatural in the midst of our trials. For this to happen, it absolutely requires the provisions of the New Covenant.

In closing, let me express my conviction that the time has come for a spiritual revolution founded upon New Covenant sanctification. I don't say this lightly or easily. This revolution will not occur overnight, nor will it go unopposed. But it is desperately needed. No one can look at the state of the church today and not agree that *something* is missing—badly missing in many cases. People are routinely either burned or bored by their experience with church; many never give Christianity a second look.

We owe it to God and to this dying world to give a clear glimpse of the true Christ through our daily lives. For this to happen, the provisions of the New Covenant are not merely good options; they are absolute essentials.

I see encouraging signs from many quarters that this revolution is beginning. It goes by different names but has one central message: Christ Himself is as much the key to sanctification as He is to justification. More and more thirsty hearts are tasting the new wine of New Covenant living, and as a result they will no longer settle for stale religiosity or dry rule-keeping.

May God mightily increase their number for the sake of His glory. May you be counted among them.

Notes

FOREWORD: LET YOUR HEART DREAM

page

ix   "It is not for your sake": Ezekiel 36:22, NIV.

CHAPTER 1: READY FOR RELEASE

page

5   "Discipleship is built": Oswald Chambers, *My Utmost for His Highest: An Updated Edition in Today's Language,* ed. James Reimann (Grand Rapids, Mich.: Discovery House Publishers, 1992), October 21.

6   "commandments are not burdensome": 1 John 5:3.

8   "substantial healing": Francis A. Schaeffer, *True Spirituality* (Wheaton, Ill.: Tyndale, 1971), 134.

9   "new covenant" (first mention); "not according to" old: Jeremiah 31:31-32. One of the central issues about such Old Testament passages as this one is how this New Covenant applies to the church today. Clearly the promises of the New Covenant were originally addressed to the nation of Israel. How can the church then legitimately claim these promises for herself? The issue is complex, and in this brief setting I will highlight only two significant points in my understanding of it: (1) The promises of the New Covenant will find their ultimate and complete fulfillment with the nation of Israel in what is commonly referred to as the "millennial kingdom." However, the church enters now into a strong foretaste of the New Covenant's spiritual blessings. Like the kingdom of God, the New Covenant is "now, but not yet." (2) New Testament authors as well as Jesus Himself provide us more than sufficient warrant for

applying to ourselves the spiritual blessings of the New Covenant. In Luke 22:20 we find Christ's unmistakable assertion that the New Covenant was about to be inaugurated through His death: "This cup is the new covenant in My blood, which is shed for you." Other references in the New Testament that indicate or imply our present participation in the New Covenant include Romans 2:28-29; 2 Corinthians 3:1-18 and 6:16; Galatians 3:13-14, 5:6, and 6:15; Philippians 3:3; Colossians 2:11-12; Hebrews 7:18-22, 8:6-13, 9:15, 10:9-25, and 12:24; and many others.

10   "No one sews": Mark 2:21-22.

12   "sinful passions were aroused": Romans 7:5.

12   "that you may be married": Romans 7:4.

13   "The law demands": Pascal, *Pensées,* Everyman edition (New York: Dutton, 1958), pensée #521, page 142.

14   Watchword is God's "I will": Jeremiah 31:33-34; Ezekiel 36:25-27.

15   "bear fruit": Romans 7:4.

15   "we should serve": Romans 7:6.

15   "fragrance of Christ," "aroma of life": 2 Corinthians 2:15-16.

15   "better covenant," "better promises," "better hope": Hebrews 7:22; 8:6; 7:19.

16   approaches to spiritual maturity: Larry Crabb, *Connecting* (Nashville: Word, 1997), 39.

17   "rivers of living water": John 7:38.

17   Charles Spurgeon's story of poor woman: Charles Haddon Spurgeon, *All of Grace,* Whitaker House edition (Springdale, Pa.: Whitaker, 1981), 7.

Chapter 2: First Things First: A Reputation at Stake

page

19   "Put first things first": C. S. Lewis, *Letters of C. S. Lewis,* ed. Walter Hooper and W. H. Lewis (New York: Harcourt, Brace, 1966), 228; letter of 23 April 1951, par. 2.

20   "on the side of the North": Abraham Lincoln, as quoted
      in Rev. Matthew Simpson, *Funeral Address Delivered at the
      Burial of President Lincoln* (New York: Carlton & Porter,
      1865), 16.

22   "By those who come near Me": Leviticus 10:3.

22   "they did not glorify Him": Romans 1:21.

22   "to the praise of His glory": Ephesians 1:6,12,14.

22   "in all things God may be glorified": 1 Peter 4:11.

23   "Whatever you do": 1 Corinthians 10:31.

23   biblical images of glory (blinding light, etc.): Acts 22:11, NIV;
      Exodus 24:17; Psalm 29:3-4; Ezekiel 1:13,28.

23   "everyone…called by My name": Isaiah 43:7.

23   "formed for Myself": Isaiah 43:21.

23   "You lead Your people": Isaiah 63:14.

24   "kingdom of priests…holy nation": Exodus 19:6.

24   "chosen generation…royal priesthood": 1 Peter 2:9.

25   Henry Stanley on David Livingstone, as quoted in Ruth A. Tucker,
      From Jerusalem to Irian Jaya (Grand Rapids, Mich.: Zondervan,
      1983), 153.

25   "first duty": John Calvin: as quoted in Charles W. Colson,
      Loving God (Grand Rapids, Mich.: Zondervan, 1983), 176.

26   "profaned My holy name": Ezekiel 36:20.

26   "I poured out My fury": Ezekiel 36:18.

27   "should also be beautiful": Francis Schaeffer, *True Spirituality*
      (Wheaton, Ill.: Tyndale, 1971), 177.

27   "faith working through love": Galatians 5:6.

28   "best argument": Sheldon Vanauken, *A Severe Mercy* (San
      Francisco: Harper & Row, 1977), 85.

28   "concern" for His name: Ezekiel 36:21.

28   Pharaoh's daughter's compassion: Exodus 2:6.

29   "I will take you…I will cleanse you": Ezekiel 36:24-27.

29   "for My holy name's sake": Ezekiel 36:22.

29   every knee…"Jesus Christ is Lord": Philippians 2:10-11.

30   "Put first things first": Lewis, *Letters of C. S. Lewis,* 228.

CHAPTER 3: BECOMING SPIRITUALLY PROVOCATIVE

page

32   "conformed to the image": Romans 8:29.

33   John the Baptist preaching and responding to various groups' questions: Luke 3:10-14.

34   "adorn the doctrine": Titus 2:10.

34   "day of visitation": 1 Peter 2:12.

35   "Hallowed be Your name": Matthew 6:9-10.

35   "godly offspring": Malachi 2:15.

36   "His workmanship": Ephesians 2:10.

36   "Every disability": C. S. Lewis in a letter to Sheldon Vanauken, as quoted in Sheldon Vanauken, *A Severe Mercy* (San Francisco: Harper & Row, 1977), 147.

37   "how to use God": As related to me by Walt Baker, missions professor at Dallas Theological Seminary, from a personal conversation with Dr. Eugene Nida.

38   "woe" upon others: Isaiah 5:18,20-22.

38   Isaiah sees the Lord: 6:1-5.

39   David to Goliath, 1 Samuel 17:45.

39   Jesus cleansing the temple, "Zeal for Your house": John 2:13-17.

39   "transformed…from glory to glory"; "beholding as in a mirror": 2 Corinthians 3:18.

40   "simultaneous consummation": John Piper, *The Supremacy of God in Preaching* (Grand Rapids, Mich.: Baker, 1990), 26.

CHAPTER 4: THE JOURNEY TO RADICAL DEPENDENCE

page

42   "profits nothing": John 6:63.

44   "we will hear and do": Deuteronomy 5:27.

44   "such a heart": Deuteronomy 5:29.

44   "circumcise your heart": Deuteronomy 30:6.

45   "darkened": Romans 1:21.

45   "various lusts": Titus 3:3.

45   "to his own way": Isaiah 53:6.

45   "none who seeks": Romans 3:11.

45   "mud pies": C. S. Lewis, "The Weight of Glory," in *The Weight of Glory and Other Addresses* (1949; reprint, New York: Macmillan, 1980), 4.

47   "God looks down": Psalm 53:2-3.

47   "none righteous": Romans 3:10.

47   "cleanse ourselves": 2 Corinthians 7:1.

47   "sins of the flesh": C. S. Lewis, *Mere Christianity* (New York: Macmillan, 1960), 94-95.

48   prodigal son parable: Luke 15:11-32.

48   "All the tax collectors": Luke 15:1-2.

49   "drunken peasant": Martin Luther, as quoted in *What Luther Says,* comp. Ewald M. Plass (St. Louis: Concordia, 1959), 1533.

50   unresolved anger: Matthew 5:21-22.

50   adultery in heart: Matthew 5:27-28.

50   "fall short": Romans 3:23.

51   "without Me": John 15:5.

51   "In whatever you judge another": Romans 2:1.

52   "so many recesses": John Calvin, *Institutes,* trans. Henry Beveridge (Grand Rapids, Mich.: Eerdmans, 1962), 478.

53   "heart to know Me": Jeremiah 24:7.

53   "new heart...new spirit": Ezekiel 36:26.

CHAPTER 5: RELEASING YOUR NEW PURITY

page

55   "from God in God": A. W. Tozer, *The Knowledge of the Holy* (San Francisco: Harper & Row, 1961), 114.

55   George Wilson story, *United States v Wilson,* 32 U.S. 150, 7 Pet. 150, 8 L.Ed. 640 (U.S.Pa. 1833).

56   "You shall be clean": Ezekiel 36:25.

56   "justified": Romans 5:1.

58   "rejoice over you": Zephaniah 3:17.

58   "hidden with Christ": Colossians 3:3.

58   "My beloved Son": Matthew 3:17.

59   "remember no more": Jeremiah 31:34.

59   "no more death, nor sorrow": Revelation 21:4.

59   "eucatastrophe": J. R. R. Tolkien, "On Fairy-Stories," *Tree and Leaf* (1964; reprint, New York: Houghton Mifflin, 1989), 62.

60   "Most assuredly": John 5:24.

60   "I give them eternal life"; "My Father"; "shall never perish": John 10:28-29.

61   "lest anyone should boast": Ephesians 2:8-9.

61   "given us eternal life…that you may know": 1 John 5:11-13.

62   "from dead works": Hebrews 9:14.

62   "garments of salvation": Isaiah 61:10.

63   "grace abounded": Romans 5:20.

63   "hearts sprinkled": Hebrews 10:22.

64   "from all sin": 1 John 1:7.

65   "grandfather in Heaven": C. S. Lewis, *The Problem of Pain* (New York: Macmillan, 1962), 28.

66   "God dwells in light": Martin Luther, as quoted in Roland Bainton, *Here I Stand* (Nashville: Abingdon, 1950), 43.

66   "God of White-Hot Rage": John White, *The Race* (Downers Grove, Ill.: InterVarsity, 1984), 25, 33.

67   "God to manageable terms": A. W. Tozer, *The Knowledge of the Holy* (San Francisco: Harper & Row, 1961), 10.

68   John's vision of Lion and Lamb: Revelation 5:5-6.

69   R. C. Sproul on Jonathan Edwards's sermon: R. C. Sproul, *The Holiness of God* (Wheaton, Ill.: Tyndale, 1988), 224.

69   "everlasting fire": Matthew 18:8.

69   "not quenched": Mark 9:43-48.

69   Abraham, Lazarus, and rich man: Luke 16:19-31.

69   "everlasting destruction": 2 Thessalonians 1:9.

70   "worm does not die": Mark 9:48.

70   "It would be dreadful": Jonathan Edwards, "Sinners in the Hands

of an Angry God," *The Works of Jonathan Edwards* (Edinburgh: The Banner of Truth and Trust, 1834), 11.

71 "Jesus paid it all": lyrics by Robert Lowry.

CHAPTER 6: DANGEROUS—AND WORTH THE RISK

page

72 "Then suddenly there dawns": Paul Tournier, *Guilt and Grace,* trans. Arthur W. Heathcote (San Francisco: Harper & Row, 1983), 193.

75 prodigal son parable: Luke 15:11-32.

78 "accepted in the Beloved": Ephesians 1:6.

78 "What shall we say": Romans 6:1-2.

78 "How shall we who died to sin": Romans 6:2.

79 "a very good test": D. Martyn Lloyd-Jones, *Romans: An Exposition of Chapter 6* (Grand Rapids, Mich.: Zondervan, 1972), 8.

79 "grace...into lewdness": Jude 4.

80 "what manner of love": 1 John 3:1.

80 "as You have loved Me": John 17:23.

81 "the 'yes' of the heart": Martin Luther, as quoted in *What Luther Says,* comp. Ewald M. Plass (St. Louis: Concordia, 1959), 1376.

81 "Blessed are the poor in spirit": Matthew 5:3.

82 "For Christ is the end": Romans 10:4.

82 "Faith consists": J. Gresham Machen, *What Is Faith?* (Edinburgh: The Banner of Truth and Trust, 1925), 178.

84 "fornicators," "idolaters," etc.; "But you were washed": 1 Corinthians 6:9-11.

84 "common or unclean": Acts 10:28.

CHAPTER 7: RELEASING YOUR NEW IDENTITY

page

86 "continue in sin": Romans 6:1.

87 "you received the Spirit of adoption": Romans 8:15.

87   "by nature children of wrath": Ephesians 2:3.

87   "partakers of the divine nature": 2 Peter 1:4.

88   "regeneration and renewing": Titus 3:5.

88   costume jewelry or tarnished silver: I first heard this illustration from Robert Oliver, a good friend and pastor of Bastrop Bible Church.

90   "You are in Christ"; what Christ "became for us": 1 Corinthians 1:30.

90   "hidden with Christ": Colossians 3:3-4.

92   "inherent as well as imputed": Jonathan Edwards, *Jonathan Edwards: Basic Writings*, ed. Ola Elizabeth Winslow (New York: Penguin, 1966), 107.

92   "actual deliverance": Edwards, *Jonathan Edwards: Basic Writings*, 107.

93   "He who glories": 1 Corinthians 1:31.

93   "crucified with Christ": Galatians 2:20.

93   "born crucified": L. E. Maxwell, *Born Crucified* (Chicago: Moody, 1945), 7.

93   "old man was crucified": Romans 6:6.

94   "Reckon yourselves": Romans 6:11.

94   "Sin need have no more power": Ruth Paxson, as quoted in Miles J. Stanford, *The Complete Green Letters* (Grand Rapids, Mich.: Zondervan, 1975), 50.

94   "buried with Him": Colossians 2:12.

94   "Old things have passed away": 2 Corinthians 5:17.

95   "created according to God": Ephesians 4:24.

95   "raised with Christ": Colossians 3:1.

95   "Just as Christ was raised": Romans 6:4.

96   "no longer I who live": Galatians 2:20.

96   "always lives to make intercession": Hebrews 7:25.

96   "The life that once He lived": anonymous.

CHAPTER 8: YOUR NEWNESS GOES PUBLIC

page

98   "God became man": C. S. Lewis, *Mere Christianity* (New York: Macmillan, 1960), 182.

100	"complete in Him": Colossians 2:10.
101	only accurate labels: 1 Corinthians 1:30; 2 Corinthians 5:17; 2 Peter 1:4; Colossians 2:10; 2 Corinthians 2:15; Ephesians 2:10; Romans 8:16,17,37.
103	"Should anyone knock": Martin Luther, as quoted in J. Oswald Sanders, *Paul the Leader* (Colorado Springs, Colo.: NavPress, 1984), 74.
104	"such were some of you": 1 Corinthians 6:11.
105	"walk in newness of life": Romans 6:4.
105	"end of those things is death": Romans 6:21.
106	"angel trapped inside": Michelangelo, as quoted in *Sunday Sermons Treasury of Illustrations,* comp. James F. Colaianni (Pleasantville, N.J.: Voicings, 1982), 532.

CHAPTER 9: RELEASING YOUR NEW DISPOSITION

page

108	"When the law is written": Andrew Murray, *The Two Covenants* (1898; reprint, Fort Washington, Pa.: Christian Literature Crusade, 1974), 117-118.
109	"holy, heavenly disposition": Jonathan Edwards, as quoted in *Closer Walk New Testament,* ed. Dr. Bruce H. Wilkinson (Grand Rapids, Mich.: Zondervan, 1990), 498.
109	"heart of stone": Ezekiel 36:26.
109	"alienated from the life of God": Ephesians 4:18.
109	"Enmity against God": Romans 8:7.
110	"a new heart...a heart of flesh": Ezekiel 36:26.
111	"I will put My law in their minds": Jeremiah 31:33.
111	"epistle"; "not on tablets of stone": 2 Corinthians 3:3.
111	"not with ink": 2 Corinthians 3:3.
112	"implanted word"; "with meekness": James 1:21.
112	"we have the mind of Christ": 1 Corinthians 2:16.
112	"are not burdensome": 1 John 5:3.
113	"love one another": John 13:34-35.

113   "Concerning brotherly love": 1 Thessalonians 4:9.

113   remain sexually pure: 1 Thessalonians 4:3; 1 Corinthians 6:18.

114   "Human nature, if it is healthy": Oswald Chambers, as quoted in
       Refresh, Renew, Revive, ed. H. B. London Jr. (Colorado Springs,
       Colo.: Focus on the Family, 1996), 73-74.

115   "circumcise your heart…to love": Deuteronomy 30:6.

116   "I will put My fear in their hearts": Jeremiah 32:40.

116   "a heart to know Me": Jeremiah 24:7.

117   "the work of the law": Romans 2:15.

117   "moral consciousness…inherent": Renald Showers, *The New
       Nature* (Neptune, N.J.: Loizeaux Brothers, 1986), 48.

118   "The moment we believe": J. Oswald Sanders, *Spiritual Lessons,*
       rev. ed. (Chicago: Moody, 1971), 105.

119   "Well done": Matthew 25:21.

Chapter 10: Both Faith and Feelings

page

120   "The sense I had of divine things": Jonathan Edwards, *Jonathan
       Edwards: Basic Writings,* ed. Ola Elizabeth Winslow (New York:
       Penguin, 1966), 84.

121   "in large part" of true "holy affections," "always a dynamic thing":
       Jonathan Edwards, *Religious Affections* (Portland, Ore.:
       Multnomah, 1984), 8.

123   "serve the Lord with gladness": Psalm 100:2.

123   "that your joy may be full": John 15:11.

124   "My food is to do the will of Him": John 4:34.

124   "one who wills to do good": Romans 7:21.

125   "inward man," "delight": Romans 7:22.

125   "law of liberty…this one will be blessed": James 1:25.

126   "Exercise yourself toward godliness": 1 Timothy 4:7.

126   "Desire the pure milk": 1 Peter 2:2.

127   pray "in the Spirit," "with all perseverance": Ephesians 6:18.

127   "draw near": Hebrews 10:22.

127   "get ahold of God": Oswald Chambers, *My Utmost for His Highest: An Updated Edition in Today's Language,* ed. James Reimann (Grand Rapids, Mich.: Discovery House Publishers, 1992), February 7.

127   "makes God real": R. A. Torrey, *How to Pray* (Springdale, Pa.: Whitaker, 1983), 13.

127   "True prayer": Samuel Zwemer, *Into all the World* (Grand Rapids, Mich.: Zondervan, 1943), 160.

127   "perfect, overflowing, unutterable happiness": Charles Spurgeon, as quoted in J. O. Sanders, *The Divine Art of Soul-Winning* (n.p., 1937).

127   "no one according to the flesh": 2 Corinthians 5:16.

128   "Through Christ toward God": 2 Corinthians 3:4.

Chapter 11: Releasing Your New Power

page

130   "New Testament Christianity": Martyn Lloyd-Jones, *The Best of Martyn Lloyd-Jones,* comp. Christopher Catherwood (Grand Rapids, Mich.: Baker, 1993), 38.

131   Thomas Carlyle story: *Illustrations for Preaching,* comp. Benjamin P. Browne (Nashville: Broadman, 1977), 54-55.

131   "I will put My Spirit": Ezekiel 36:27.

132   "The letter kills": 2 Corinthians 3:6.

132   "the Spirit gives life": 2 Corinthians 3:6.

133   "Are you so foolish?": Galatians 3:3.

133   "what I am doing, I do not understand": Romans 7:15.

134   "the flesh lusts against the Spirit": Galatians 5:17.

134   "Thanks be to God...in triumph": 2 Corinthians 2:14.

134   "Walk in the Spirit": Galatians 5:16.

136   "nothing good dwells": Romans 7:18.

136   "O wretched man": Romans 7:24.

136   "I thank God—through Jesus Christ": Romans 7:25.

136   "As you therefore have received Christ": Colossians 2:6.

137   "working continuously in you": Philippians 2:13, author's translation.

138   "You shall be witnesses": Acts 1:8.

138   "complete in Christ": Colossians 1:28, NASB.

138   not anything except what Christ had accomplished: Romans 15:18.

139   "the light…in the face of Jesus Christ": 2 Corinthians 4:6.

139   "Whoever abides in Him": 1 John 3:6.

CHAPTER 12: DYNAMIC DEPENDENCE

page

140   "The Spirit is an imperative necessity": A. W. Tozer, *Man: The Dwelling Place of God* (Harrisburg, Pa.: Christian Publications, 1966), 66.

140   "It is to your advantage": John 16:7.

141   "Christ lives in me": Galatians 2:20.

141   "rivers of living water": John 7:38.

141   the vine and branches; "Abide in Me": John 15:1-8.

141   "bear fruit": John 15:2,4.

142   "I am the vine, you are the branches": John 15:5.

142   "If you do not forgive": Matthew 6:15.

142   "Leave your gift"; "Go your way": Matthew 5:23-24.

143   "and My words abide…you will ask": John 15:7.

143   "The Son can do nothing of Himself": John 5:19.

143   "Apart from Me you can do nothing": John 15:5, NASB.

145   "Do not be drunk with wine": Ephesians 5:18.

146   "led by the Spirit": Romans 8:14; Galatians 5:18.

146   "active passivity": Francis Schaeffer, *The Complete Works of Francis A. Schaeffer: A Christian Worldview,* vol. 3, *A Christian View of Spirituality* (Wheaton, Ill.: Crossway, 1982), 281.

147   "fruit of the Spirit": Galatians 5:22-23.

Chapter 13: A Fresh Look at Intimacy with God

page

149   "He meant us to see Him": A. W. Tozer, *The Pursuit of God* (Camp Hill, Pa.: Christian Publications, 1982), 34.

150   "they all shall know Me": Jeremiah 31:34.

151   "flesh and blood has not revealed": Matthew 16:17.

151   "fountain of water": John 4:14.

151   "leaping": Acts 3:8; 14:10.

152   "filled with the Spirit": Ephesians 5:18.

153   "speaking to one another in psalms": Ephesians 5:19-20.

153   "by Him let us continually offer": Hebrews 13:15.

153   "Spirit of adoption": Romans 8:15; see also Galatians 4:6.

154   "We do not know what we should pray": Romans 8:26.

154   "Christian mysticism": Francis Schaeffer, *True Spirituality* (Wheaton, Ill.: Tyndale, 1971), 54-55, 69-70.

155   "You flashed, You shone": Augustine, "The Confessions of St. Augustin," *A Select Library of the Nicene and Post-Nicene Fathers of the Christian Church,* ed. Philip Schaff (Grand Rapids, Mich.: Eerdmans, 1979), XXVII: 38.

Chapter 14: A Fresh Look at Freedom in Christ

page

157   "A Christian is a perfectly free": Martin Luther, "The Freedom of a Christian," *Three Treatises* (Philadelphia: Fortress, 1943), 277.

157   "means different things to different people": Eugene Peterson, *Traveling Light* (Colorado Springs: Helmers & Howard, 1988), 57-58.

158   "free indeed": John 8:36.

158   "Where the Spirit of the Lord is": 2 Corinthians 3:17.

159   "You may be able to compel people": Reinhold Niebuhr, as quoted in Charles R. Swindoll, *The Grace Awakening* (Nashville: Word, 1990), xv.

159   "Stand fast therefore": Galatians 5:1.

159   "Do not use liberty": Galatians 5:13.

160   "prisms refracting the light": John Piper, *Desiring God* (Portland, Ore.: Multnomah, 1986), 43.

160   "A slave is a living tool": Aristotle, *Nicomachean Ethics,* trans. and ed., Roger Crisp (Cambridge: Cambridge University Press, 2000), 158.

161   "Having been set free": Romans 6:18.

161   "the Son makes you free": John 8:36.

162   "a slave of sin": John 8:34.

162   "The law of the Spirit of life": Romans 8:2.

162   "through love serve one another": Galatians 5:13-14.

163   "perfectly free lord of all": Luther, *Three Treatises,* 277.

164   "weak": 1 Corinthians 8:9-12.

164   Galatians, their joy evaporated, etc.: see Galatians 1:7; 3:1; 4:13-15; 5:1,15.

CHAPTER 15: A FRESH LOOK AT COMMUNITY

page

167   "our care for the helpless": Tertullian, *Apologetical Works* (Washington, D.C.: Catholic University of America Press, 1950), 99.

168   disconnected from ourselves and others: Francis Schaeffer, *The Complete Works of Francis A. Schaeffer: A Christian Worldview,* vol. 3, *A Christian View of Spirituality* (Wheaton, Ill.: Crossway, 1982), 373-374.

169   "I will give them one heart": Jeremiah 32:39.

169   "Christian brotherhood": Dietrich Bonhoeffer, *Life Together* (San Francisco: Harper & Row, 1954), 30.

169   "keep the unity of the Spirit": Ephesians 4:3.

170   "increase and abound in love": 1 Thessalonians 3:12.

171   Larry Crabb, ministry and manipulation: Lawrence J. Crabb Jr. and Dan B. Allender, *Encouragement: The Key to Caring* (Grand Rapids, Mich.: Zondervan, 1984), 96.

CHAPTER 16: A FRESH LOOK AT MINISTRY

183	"His workmanship": Ephesians 2:10.
183	"Out of his heart": John 7:38.
184	love one another: John 13:34.
184	"to the end": John 13:1.
184	"bears all things"; "never fails": 1 Corinthians 13:7-8.
186	"not by might": Zechariah 4:6.
186	"the Son can do nothing of Himself": John 5:19.
186	"My Father has been working": John 5:17.
186	"I can of Myself do nothing": John 5:30.
186	"The Father who dwells in Me": John 14:10.
187	"As the Father has sent Me": John 20:21.
187	cloud and a pillar of fire: Exodus 13:21; Numbers 14:14.
188	"calls His own sheep by name": John 10:3-4.
189	"Do you not know that your bodies": 1 Corinthians 6:15-16.
190	as Nathan did for David: 2 Samuel 12.
191	"steal no longer"; "Rather let him labor": Ephesians 4:28.

Acknowledgments

This book would never have been possible without the sacrifice, support, and encouragement of my wonderful family—my wife, Sandy, and our three fine sons, Stephen, Jordan, and Brandon. What a blessed man I am!

I also would like to express my deep gratitude to the elders, staff, and saints of Grace Bible Church in College Station, Texas. You have so richly blessed us over these past twenty years. How privileged I am to help pastor such choice servants of God.

Above all else, I want to thank Jesus Christ, who has brought me out of the miry clay, set my feet upon the Rock, and put a new song in my mouth. This book is in large measure that song.